ADDICTED LIKE ME

A Mother-Daughter Story of Substance Abuse and Recovery

KAREN FRANKLIN AND
LAUREN KING

SEAL PRESS

ADDICTED LIKE ME
A Mother-Daughter Story of Substance Abuse and Recovery

Published by
Seal Press
A Member of the Perseus Books Group
1700 Fourth Street
Berkeley, California

Library of Congress Cataloging-in-Publication Data

Franklin, Karen, 1955-
    Addicted like me : a mother-daughter story of substance abuse and recovery / Karen Franklin and Lauren King.
        p. cm.
    ISBN 978-1-58005-286-3
    1. Franklin, Karen, 1955– 2. King, Lauren, 1980– 3. Recovering addicts—United States—Biography. 4. Addicts—Family relationships—United States. 5. Addicts—Rehabilitation—United States. 6. Substance abuse—Treatment—United States. I. King, Lauren, 1980– II. Title.
    HV4998.F73 2009
    362.29092'273—dc22
    [B]
                                    2009004843

Cover and Interior design by Domini Dragoone
Printed in the United States of America by Edwards Brothers
Distributed by Publishers Group West

To respect the privacy of individuals mentioned in the book, the authors have changed some names.

TO JASON AND RICK.
We'll keep the light on.

CONTENTS

PART I.

WATCHING MY ADDICTION CLAIM MY KIDS

A Mother's Story of Inherited Addiction and Abuse

PART II.

WATCHING MYSELF FALL
A Daughter's Story of Beating the Legacy of Addiction

PART III.

WATCHING US RECOVER
A Mother-Daughter Guide to Recovery Strategies and Hope

INTRODUCTION

IF YOU ARE A PERSON who is struggling with addiction, please know that you are not alone. I know this from personal experience. A thread of alcoholism that began in my family generations before I was born came to greet me on the day of my birth. It culminated with the addiction of both my teenagers. Watching Lauren and Ryan become consumed by our legacy of family addiction, I experienced a parent's worst nightmare. I occupied a front row seat, observing the self-destruction of my children through drug and alcohol abuse. I lived in constant fear. I believed that my daughter, Lauren, would never live to see her eighteenth birthday because her addiction was so out of control at one point. In *Addicted Like Me*, Lauren and I tell our own stories, though my story invariably involves my own ups and downs and challenges and victories, as well as those of my children. Ultimately ours is a story of hope and how we found recovery from the devastating heritage of addiction that has plagued our family for generations, but each of us—myself, Lauren, and Ryan—is testimony to the fact that addiction is not an easy cycle to break. Awareness is the first, all-important step. No matter what stage you're facing—be it coming to terms with your family history, your own impact on your child's addiction, their downward spiral, or their long-awaited recovery—being willing to face it, with your eyes wide open, and having the desire to effect change in your situation is what makes all the difference.

I was thrilled when Lauren agreed to coauthor this book with me. I knew then that both of our voices needed to be shared. I believe that Lauren's telling of her own side of the story gives this book a powerful dimension that will help parents who are struggling for understanding, and will resonate with young people searching for a way out.

In telling our story, Lauren and I have ripped our souls bare. In the first two parts of the book we relive very difficult and painful periods in our lives. In the third part, we let you in on the strategies that lead to our success so that you are able to put yourself in the shoes of a teenager or a parent.

As I look back on the insanity of it all before Lauren and I embraced recovery, I wonder how I coped as a single parent. I did everything I could think of to try to stop addiction from consuming her and my son, but in the end, I had to admit I was absolutely powerless. Addiction is the responsibility of each individual. The hope to recover from addiction is in the choice you can make as an individual to change. This realization finally hit me when I recognized I had been standing on a set of train tracks with outstretched arms trying to stop a speeding train. As defeated as I felt, it was the turning point in our family's recovery. I let go of trying to control what could not be controlled, and it was then that we began to find solutions.

Addiction is a disease that is deadly and serious. It is not a habit. I needed to learn as much as I could about this illness to help my family. When it comes to addiction, a lack of knowledge can be a recipe for disaster. All of us owe it to our kids to become informed. Most important, I discovered success after I reached out for help. Most parents feel that they should be able to get their kids under control, and I was no exception. The problem is that we are up against something powerful and insidious in addiction, and we need one another. You will need all the help you can get to achieve a successful recovery. The knowledge and support of others will become a power for you, as they have been and continue to be for me.

Having an adult relationship with my children, who have suffered in very different ways, has opened a door into so many things I ignored or tried to wish away while they were growing up. But that approach only made the problems bigger. I had no clue that many things I was doing or not doing were allowing Lauren and Ryan to continue with their addictions. With all of the good intentions in the world, I was enabling them. I was unable to recognize the role I played in our legacy of addiction because I had tolerated unacceptable, addicted behavior for so long. My grandfather was an addict and so was my father, as was the first man I married, Rick. I was perpetuating this legacy by living in denial of the fact that it had come to live in my children.

Coming out of denial was painful, but I learned that denial is a dangerous place to be if you are the parent of an addict. The National Institute on Drug Abuse released some startling numbers for 2007. The numbers vary by year, and different drugs seem to fall in and out of favor with experimenting youths, but one thing always stays the same—more teens than not are trying drugs and alcohol.

Alcohol: 72 percent of teens surveyed by the National Institute had used alcohol, 66 percent used within one year of the survey, and 44 percent used within that month.

Marijuana: Nearly 42 percent of teens reported that they had tried the drug, 32 used within one year of the survey, and 19 used within that month.

Prescription pain pills: 15 percent of high school seniors reported having used prescription painkillers to get high during the twelve months preceding the National Institute survey.

The consequences that our children are experiencing from drinking and drug use can be astonishing. Their judgment becomes impaired when they are under the influence of drugs and alcohol, and they make choices that have severe repercussions. The survey found that sexual encounters with risks of pregnancy, STDs, and HIV exposure, as well as date rape and other violence, can and do occur more frequently while young people are consuming large amounts of alcohol by binge drinking. These behaviors also lead to unwanted pregnancies, sexually transmitted diseases, and depression. Physical fighting and abuse can lead to major issues, including problems with the law. These repercussions are just the tip of the iceberg as far as statistics go but certainly make a strong case for why our children need our help. Lauren could not help herself. She and I had to work as a team to put our likelihood of risk and repercussion to rest.

As my understanding of addictive realities progressed, I poured all of my energies into bettering myself so that I might help my children. I didn't know things could be different for a family like mine until I was introduced to the information I had been lacking, the support I needed from others, and the encouragement that helped change my perception. Lauren and I want to be that encouragement for you. We have been through similar situations. We have felt similar things. We experienced a miracle and want you to have that experience, too.

I am not a professional, but I have discovered solutions that work. As I observe my children as they face their own challenges, I continue to hope that the foundations of recovery that they learned along the way will be remembered. The road to recovery can be a bumpy journey, full of relapses and bubbles of hope that often burst. *Addicted Like Me* is about my and Lauren's experiences, but Ryan's own journey plays a significant role, too. As of the writing of this book, Lauren believes she is an addict and continues on with her recovery program; Ryan feels that he is not an addict, and that his previous addictions do not affect his life today. As their parent, there were things I could have done better, and you, reader, must not despair if the techniques and suggestions we provide at the end of the book don't work for you or your child. Sometimes the road to recovery takes years and years, and these solutions are not a template for success. This is our story, however, and it's one in which Lauren and I share with you our journey to recovery as a team. You are not alone. Don't ever give up on your child. You need one another to break the legacy of addiction. It is a beast, and it is powerful, but it is never as strong as the bond you can build in your family by breaking free into recovery together.

—KAREN FRANKLIN
2009

• • •

IT WAS HEARTBREAKING when I finally opened my eyes and saw that I was the cause of so much of my family's pain. My mother was overwhelmed and scared. She ran around during the years I was an addict like a chicken with her head cut off, constantly grasping at straws in an effort to reach out to me. She was never able to rest or relax, because she was always worried about the next big bomb. When would it drop on us because of my addiction? Everything she tried to change for my brother and me would come crashing down, leaving shambles.

It was an absolutely devastating time for our family. My mom had cleaned up her own addictions years before I began to lose myself to the same beast that had consumed her. Tension was off the charts. My mood swings were outrageous. My mother walked on eggshells, wanting so much to bring me the healing that she had found, but I had constant anger toward her for interfering with my life.

I met every opportunity for change that she presented to me with a fight. I had no idea this resistance was a part of my disease. Addiction tries to find any way it can to survive and thrive. When I was confronted about my addictions, it only intensified my anger and the burden I felt from carrying so much rage around. It created a pressure inside me that nearly drove me crazy. I medicated myself with drugs and alcohol to cover up the pain I felt, meanwhile causing everyone I came in contact with to suffer.

As a teen, I tried any high that came my way. I didn't discriminate against any drug. It didn't start out that way, but year after year I found myself more willing to try anything, and do anything, for a high. When I began using drugs and alcohol, I withdrew from my life. It seemed inevitable, and is now evident, that the beast of addiction was devouring me.

My thinking was altered after I lost myself to addiction. Lying became a priority to keep addiction the most important thing in my world. I found myself willing to hide my secret at any cost. If you are living with an addict, you have to remember that you are up against secrecy, shame, and an intense desire to retreat from everything, even the healing that you may be yearning for underneath it all.

My mother first approached me with the idea of writing this book many years ago. Initially, I was excited to start the project, but once I began to write I found it draining to relive the nightmare we had experienced together. Feelings of regret engulfed me. I began to think about all the pain I caused my family. I feel deep remorse for the people who crossed my path during the time that addictions ruled my life. I may have influenced many people to try drugs and alcohol. It has become my mission to right this wrong, to write this book, and to speak out about recovery. I want to give others the hope I was given as a tribute to every person I may have victimized.

In my section of this book, I take you through the journey of teen addiction and how it came to take over my life. I try my best to remember the feelings I was experiencing, and the justifications I made up, to give you an idea of how a drug user thinks. There were times while writing about this part of my life that I didn't think I would be able to finish sharing the sort of person I used to be. I had doubts about opening myself up to admit my failures, mistakes, and vulnerabilities. However, the fact is that no one can tell my story better than I can. Let my story begin to show you the way.

Anybody can sit and point the finger and say an addict has to change. It wasn't until I was shown how to start making changes, and the people around me began to educate themselves, that I was able to make the decision to hope I could be different. It didn't take just my willpower to choose hope; I also needed to be shown that I was worth believing in. It has not been easy to believe in myself. Faith in my own personal power to remain sober is something that I will always be working on, just as you will if you begin recovery by reading this book.

In recovery you can expect to sit in the front row of your own life instead of hiding in the back, withdrawn. I think about my own two children and the world they are growing up in. I wonder if they will experience the same addictions I faced because our addiction is a family legacy. I wonder if the beast of addiction will wake in the next generation and become stronger, or if my mother and I have tamed the beast for good. These are questions that can only be answered with time. It is now my turn to educate, and my time to protect my children, and to engage others in a conversation about the road out of addiction and toward recovery. I am proof that a legacy of addiction can be broken, even if it is a family affair that has lasted for years.

—LAUREN KING

2009

PART I

WATCHING MY ADDICTION CLAIM MY KIDS

A Mother's Story of Inherited
Addiction and Abuse

AN ADDICT'S LIFE

CHAPTER 1

AT AN EARLY AGE I learned unconsciously that the way to cope with life was to abuse substances. My grandfather abused alcohol and then abandoned my father and his siblings. My father abused alcohol and then abused our family. After my mother passed away from cancer, my sister married and moved, and my brother joined the Air Force. I was left alone to receive my father's rage. At first I abused food but quickly turned to abusing other substances to numb my pain.

I remember taking my first drink at thirteen years old. A girlfriend invited me to go drinking with the crowd she was hanging around with. Because I didn't know what effect drinking would have on me, I was insecure about the invite. The night before we were supposed to go out with her friends, I decided to do a trial run. At home alone I drank two big glasses of vodka and orange juice. I felt numb, but only a little dizzy. I felt relieved, like I could do it. It was essential for me to appear as if I knew what I was doing because of my hunger to be accepted. It was propelling me into a state of internalized mental and emotional anguish to live alone with an alcoholic father who was prone to heated rages after the death of my mom. I was lonely, chronically distressed, and full of shame.

I felt that somehow my life situation was my fault. I desperately needed the acceptance of my peers because I felt so bad about myself most of the time. I wanted to be viewed as normal and put together by the outside world. I had learned I could handle a night out with friends drinking from my trial run. It was not going to be a big deal, and I wouldn't be made fun of. I knew that if someone were to make fun of me, it would just confirm my suspicions of what I already thought about myself, which wasn't worth the risk.

The next night a group of us went to a park where some boys showed up and brought the alcohol. I was pretty confident from my previous experience, so I acted like a pro. I don't remember anything after being at that park because I blacked out. The next thing I knew it was morning. I woke up in my girlfriend's bedroom, the room spinning, and she told me I'd been hysterically funny the night before. She also told me I had gotten really wasted and thrown up several times in a car. The boys had dropped us at her house, and she had had a heck of a time getting me up the stairs to her bedroom.

That was just one step in my process of becoming addicted. I started smoking a year before, at twelve, smoking marijuana at fourteen years old, and taking hard drugs at fifteen. I became bolder as an addict, and I liked it. Because I had experienced disappointment so often growing up with my alcoholic father, my expectations had always been for the worst. My fears would grow inside me until they permeated my entire being. Once I got into drugs, I felt less fear. I spent most of my time away from my father. I stayed out at friends' houses to party on the weekends, and it was a relief to be rarely home.

When I was home, I began to stand up to my father's drunken rages. I also began to lie and steal. I would later see the same signs of boldness in my daughter and son, Lauren and Ryan, as their addictions progressed. At fourteen I stole my first painkillers from my father. His pills had been prescribed following an emergency appendicitis surgery, but he prided himself on not taking any pain medication. I think the alcohol probably did the job just as well, so his pills went untouched. He didn't miss them a bit when he returned to the house after his operation. The day he came home from the hospital, he got in the car and drove straight to the local Veterans of Foreign Wars bar, his home away from home.

I don't know how I got the brilliant idea to try his morphine pills, but I did. He had several bottles of them, and I started passing the pills out to my friends. Some days I would swallow a handful before I went to school. I felt dizzy afterward, like I might pass out and never come up to life again. At the parochial school I attended, the nun who taught my homeroom class noticed instantly that something was wrong. She took me to the convent after school one day and started to probe me for reasons. I broke down crying and told her everything about my home life. I told her it was unbearable and gave her details about what was happening between my father and me. Of course, I never mentioned the painkillers. Covering your tracks is a skill of an addict, and I was learning.

The next day my teacher met with my dad. I have no idea what she said to him, but when he came home he brought us pizza for dinner and tried to have a conversation with me, which was definitely not typical. It felt weird to have his attention, so I just played along. My father and I had so little communication outside of his screaming at me that I had no idea what to say to him. I felt so exposed. I just wanted the dinner to be over so I could go back into my bedroom and close the door to isolate and protect myself. My father and I were sinking deeper into our addictions, he into his liquor and me into my pills. We had both become reclusive when we were in our house, and the pattern that was being set would never be broken.

I grew into an addict during the 1970s, when the hippie movement was established, so drugs were flowing freely around me and rebellion was in the air. It all seemed seductive and glamorous. I was an impressionable teen, and I thought anyone drinking or doing drugs was cool. To be caught up in this high was the opposite of all the emotional pain I had locked inside. Feelings of depression, fear, and shame permeated my entire being, and I was desperate to be seen as normal. The drugs gave me the power to achieve this goal. Instantly I could numb out my distressed emotions and gain the acceptance I craved to lift my self-esteem.

During my ninth-grade year, one of my girlfriends started dating a boy who was eighteen and part of the glamorous crowd I craved to join. He and his friends were into smoking pot, and I remember it felt so special to be hanging out with really important older people, like them, who had access to drugs. After the death of my mother, I had felt only loneliness and a sense of disconnection from everyone. I missed her terribly, and I grieved the life I knew before her death. I knew my place in the world when she was alive. I felt secure. As part of this older, inner circle, I was considered cool and got that feeling back.

The first time I tried marijuana, I felt nothing. I couldn't understand what the big deal was. The second time I tried it, I felt the effect and loved it. It took the pain of life away, and I craved that release. It took the edge off, and I became a daily pot smoker, though it didn't take long before I experimented with other drugs, too. I continued stealing from my dad to fund my habit. I took money from him instead of painkillers. I would sneak into his bedroom and steal out of his wallet after he had passed out following a night at the bar. I would have risked anything to get my high at that point. I was scared to death of my father, but I would creep into his room anyway, every time I needed money. Even in broad daylight I would steal what I needed to get my fix. Sometimes I had to tiptoe inches from his slumbering body to rifle through the pockets of his pants hanging next to him on the bedpost.

I don't know if he ever knew I was doing this, but I never got caught. I never got into trouble with my father over drugs, but he did find out that I was using alcohol because I got caught drinking at a school function. This was the only time he ever hit me. I was sitting in the school cafeteria when my name was called over the intercom, which blared out the news that I was to report to the office. When I arrived I had to stand before the principal and admit everything. That's when my dad got brought into the picture. The principal said I needed to go home and tell my father about the incident because I was being suspended. I needed to bring my dad with me when I returned to school.

I knew that I couldn't tell my father what had happened. He would blow up in his usual way and maybe even more. I was unwilling to find out how much more anger I might unleash in him. For the next three days I got up and got dressed for school as if I weren't suspended, but instead of walking to school I sneaked down to the basement and hid. I sat there quietly until I heard my father leave for work. When I went back to school, the principal asked where my father was because I hadn't brought him with me. I admitted that I hadn't told my dad and just stood there waiting to see what the principal would do. I figured anything that came was better than dealing with my father's ferocity, but my hopes were dashed when I observed a sad look of resignation on the principal's face, just before he told me there was no getting around my father's anger. He was going to call my dad himself and tell him the news I hadn't.

That night I was scared to death. I waited for my father to come home, but he didn't show up until two in the morning. I heard him come in, then he opened the door to my bedroom and walked up to me. He slapped me in the face, said nothing, and walked out of my room. My cheek stung at first, but then it just felt numb. It was dark around me, and in that horror I felt completely violated at what my father had done, but soon feelings of shame and humiliation flooded over me. I turned the pain inward because I was sure it was my fault. I cried silently into my pillow, rocking myself to sleep in shame. Those were the last soundless sobs of protest I would ever make against my father.

The next time he yelled at me, I snapped. I told him I couldn't take it anymore, and that I felt like I was losing my mind. A look of fear came over his face when I finally exploded. The only time I had seen him look so fearful was when my mother lay dying. He began to sob, and then he grabbed me. My father hugged me, said he loved me, and told me he would get me some help. He said, "I love you." It's the only time I remember those words leaving my father's lips.

He promised to take me for an appointment with a psychologist, but I didn't think I was crazy. I needed something to deal with the pain we caused each other, sure, because I couldn't take the emotional battering anymore, but I didn't need a hospital. Still, he made an appointment at a mental hospital in a nearby town. My father found the hospital on a recommendation from his boss, because he also had a daughter in need of "help." As we drove up to the hospital, I noticed bars were on all the windows of the building. I was petrified that the hospital staff would keep me there and lock me up.

My father and I met with a psychologist at the hospital, together and then individually. I was taken back there several more times, and I remember the psychologist telling me that our situation was not my fault. This was well and good, but it didn't change anything at home. I don't even know if I ever really believed her when she said that the problems with my dad were not my fault. I felt ashamed and humiliated after every one of his rages at me. Maybe some of the shameful things he said about me were true. It was hard for me to differentiate fact from fiction. Even though I knew in my mind that most of the things my father said to me were not true, his hurtful words penetrated my heart and trapped themselves forever into my very being.

Eventually we stopped the hospital appointments. I never knew why, but years later my sister told me that the visits were stopped because my father must have decided he didn't want to take me there anymore. The vice principal at my high school had called my sister, in Florida, because the hospital contacted him with concerns about me after my father and I stopped our appointments. The hospital had tried to contact my father, but he never returned the calls.

This was when my father remarried. I was in high school when he and Nora wed. She was a hard woman who was unkind to me. She could drink my father under the table, but the good news was that after my dad met Nora, he stopped his drunken rages in the night. This didn't stop all the chaos, though, because Nora and I did not get along. Sometimes out of nowhere she would accuse me of things I hadn't done, like the time she accused me of stealing her car and going joyriding. I didn't even know how to drive. When I tried to defend myself against her wild stories, Nora would tell me she "had my number," and not to mess with her. Some nights when she and my father came home from the bar, I could hear Nora asking my dad if he loved her more than me.

I overheard a lot of what my father and Nora talked about. Over the years I heard some pretty hurtful things. I felt so alone and unloved. I remember hiding in the corner of my closet in the dark with the door shut so they couldn't hear me sobbing. If I could hear them, I knew they could hear me, and I didn't want to appear weak. If Nora were to know how devastated I felt over the things that were said, I knew it would please her, and I wasn't going to give her the satisfaction. Somehow it felt like she was jealous of me, but I had no idea why. Maybe it was because everyone said how much I resembled my mother. I never knew.

I moved out of my father's home the day after high school graduation. After that, life was a constant party for me. A girl I worked with had a brother who had connections. We used to get crystal meth, which is a potent form of speed. I had tried speed in the form of amphetamines before that and had kind of liked the effects, but I fell madly in love with crystal meth. It gave me energy. I felt great. I could drink all night and never get drunk, I had amazing self-confidence, and I could talk for hours, feeling like I was the most interesting person in the world.

By that time I had lost interest in pot because it no longer made me feel good. I later learned that marijuana is a depressant. It slows the nervous system to a hazy halt. My switch to meth was a chemical solution to the level of addiction I had to pot, which no longer gave me the high it had at first. I just felt kind of depressed when I used pot, and I craved the same high I knew when I first experienced life on drugs. On meth it came back in spades. I was superhuman and would sometimes go for days with no sleep at all. The drawback was coming down off the high. My brain could only function so long without sleep. I felt extremely sick, depressed, and paranoid on the way down, but the high was worth the agony of coming down, so I kept using meth whenever I had the opportunity.

One weekend, my roommates and I pooled our money to purchase meth and did the drug together, staying up all night to snort lines of the stuff. We decided to attend the county fair high on meth and had a blast. We stayed high through an entire Saturday, but by Saturday night, my roommates had lost interest in the remaining stash. I stayed home alone and finished it off. I had no shutoff valve when it came to meth. As long as there were good drugs around, I would use them up until they were gone.

I never feared overdosing or any other of the potential consequences of my behavior during that time. I couldn't even fathom how someone could just walk away and say they didn't want to do any more. It wasn't in my DNA to say no, but I wasn't as superhuman as I felt. The weekend of the meth binge and the fair, I hadn't slept since the Thursday before I started doing meth with my friends. After I hit the remaining stash by myself, I began to feel sharp pains in my chest. I felt like my heart was going to burst out of my body and knew I was in trouble. It was one of those moments that are rare, when for a flashing second it became very clear that the consequences of my actions could mean life or death. I had to do something drastic to save my life, which meant possibly revealing my addictions, and yet I was able to understand that the only alternative was death. I realized I wanted to live. I

told my roommate what was happening as soon as she came home, and she immediately called an ambulance,
saving my life.

I spent the night in the hospital on an IV to counteract the drugs. The embarrassment of getting caught did not seem nearly so important by then. I worried that soon my father would appear and find me in this collapsed state, but a blessing only an addict can appreciate occurred in the hospital. I learned it was illegal to inform my dad about my condition because I was over the age of eighteen, which meant my secret was safe from him, and from the hatred of Nora, because I was a legal adult. He never found out. Still, the shock of what had almost happened to me did curb my drug use after that time. I was scared and decided to compromise with myself. I made a vow to stick with alcohol and milder drugs only, like marijuana or painkillers, because I was afraid of what drugs had done to me but not scared enough to quit.

I had only been out of my father's home and in my own apartment for a few months when I decided that maybe what I needed was a change of scenery, so I got on a plane and went to Florida, where my sister lived. Things didn't go well there. As soon as I had an opportunity to leave, I did. I was offered a position as a baby sitter for a family that was relocating, and I jumped at the chance, landing in a town in Montana, where I decided to stay. I found a job and rented an apartment there, and I made the kind of friends I thought were normal people, people that went to bars, got drunk, and did drugs. It was lonely in Montana at first. But soon I met tons of people that lived like I did. In Montana I met

Rick, my first husband. He was my drug dealer. We met because I bought drugs from him at a bar. He was one of a string of many people I began meeting to score my highs.

Rick and I were both barely twenty years old when we met. We were both into the party scene. I thought that after we were married, our habits would change and things would settle down for us. I started to slow down some, but Rick was just warming up. His drinking and drug use escalated as the years went on. I couldn't stand the fact that he had to drink constantly, and also do drugs, and we fought often about it. I justified the criticisms I had against him by believing that I had the self-control to curb my behaviors when I wanted to. Rick did not. He smoked pot and drank every day. On the weekends we partied together, because in those days I allowed myself to binge, though I no longer smoked marijuana and sensed that I was considered uncool because of this choice. It brought back all the feelings of embarrassment I had always feared. I believed that not smoking made me look weak to other people and thought they were beginning to write me off as a lightweight.

What had changed was my tolerance for the environment around Rick and me. In the early days of our marriage, we lived with addicted friends, and our house turned into a community pot smoking den. I chose not to be part of this party because I'd become a binge addict who used only on weekends, while Rick and the others at our house were feeding their daily needs. I rationalized the exclusion I felt by telling myself I wasn't an addict, like the people I knew. Addicts were people like Rick and his friends, people that had to use every day and couldn't live without their drugs. The irony of my feeling excluded was that I couldn't live without my drugs either. I was exactly the same as the people I knew. If I could have lived without drugs, I wouldn't have needed my binges.

But I did need them, so I ignored the fact that I had fallen out of the cool crowd at our house. I concentrated on the idea that my cycle of addiction was a type of intelligence other people I knew didn't have. I told myself I wasn't quite as bad off as Rick and his friends were. He and the drug users that came and went in our home, and even my father before them, they were the ones who were screwed up. Pot had never regained the first effect it had on my life, and by this time alcohol would give me bad hangovers, so I picked and chose when I was going to party to do the hard drugs that gave me the high I wanted, and only those. This habit left me isolated from the normal routine in our house of casual pot and liquor but made me feel smarter than everyone else.

I had never heard of a binge alcoholic, or addict, at that time. It was the summer I turned twenty-one. Of course I know better now. If I had known about binge behaviors, I might have been able to respond better to the news I received that my father had a stroke, but because I thought I was better than him because I wasn't an addict, I thought I could handle watching him die. After I arrived at his bedside, I was told he most likely would not live beyond a few days. The doctor had been telling him for years that if he didn't quit drinking, it was eventually going to kill him. It did. I saw my father alive and unconscious one last time in a hospital. I buried my dad back home, in a plot right next to my mom, and returned to my life with Rick. When I returned, I was just as addicted as ever to binge behaviors and lies. I didn't have a lot of emotion regarding my father's death at the time. We were never close and barely had any kind of relationship. But one sensation I remember is feeling numb about my dad. I have learned that there are several stages of grief, and the first stage is usually denial. I believe denial was the cause of the episodes in my life when I just felt numb about my dad, because I would never admit how similar I was to him. The death of my father became another grief-moment buried deep down inside of me. It was one more reason to stay addicted to my illness, to suppress my emotions the way I always had.

Pressures were mounting around Rick and me, aside from our addictions. Rick had invited a transient, who had gray hair and a beard, to live with us. Rick let him into our life because the transient was "cool" and smoked pot. I thought the man smelled like he hadn't taken a bath in a year. There was also a drug dealer in Montana who lived down the street from Rick and me. His name was Joey. He and Rick became fast friends, using our house to do IV drugs, which in my mind were for hardcore addicts only, and were as low as one could go. That wasn't me, or us. I had tolerated Rick's daily pot smoking and the constant beer drinking, but even for his level of behavior, IV drug use was where I had to draw the line for us both. In addition, Rick didn't work when we were first married. After I lost the job that had been supporting us, he flipped. He screamed at me to go get another job, but I refused until he got one first. This was about the time I found out that I was pregnant with our first child, Jason. Rick's dad had a serious talk with his son after learning this news, and it didn't take long before Rick was working at a good job.

For a brief time, I felt safe. Maybe things would start to settle down, I thought. On a weekend before I delivered our son, though, Rick and I were still at it, partying with friends that had scored a form of speed called white crosses. I took the drugs even though I knew it was not the best idea while I was pregnant. Our son Jason was born one month premature, with his lungs underdeveloped, and the doctor who delivered Jason didn't know if he would live at all. I was lucky Jason was not born with a more serious complication from my amphetamine use, and yet this scare had a sobering effect that was regrettably short-lived. Like before, when I nearly overdosed on meth at the county fair, I compromised by bingeing to believe I had control over my drug use. Sometimes either Rick or I would stay home with Jason, so the other could go out alone to the bars with friends to drink, drug, and flirt. The fights we had after Jason was born all seemed to revolve around accusations that one of us drank too much or used too many drugs, or went off to the bars without the other, yet we kept right on doing all of these things.

We had Lauren during this time. At the time of her birth, Jason was three years old. Rick announced that year that he wanted to go to Oregon, to look for a better paying job. I didn't want to travel with a newborn, but Rick insisted that we all go. On the trip he hooked up with an old drug buddy and scored amphetamines. During the drive, Rick also bought beer, mixing the speed with the liquor as he drove our car. The trip had been stressful and I just needed something to take the edge off, so I popped a pill and washed it down with a beer. I don't remember much about the acci-dent, but I do remember the car flipping through the air. The next thing I remember I was in the hospital. I had suffered a concussion and was in shock. I have been told that it was a miracle that any of us lived. We each had multiple injuries; for instance, Lauren had finger-shaped bruises that covered her body from the all places where I had gripped her so tightly. Jason had suffered a severe head injury. I was in shock when I was told he would not survive.

Just to listen to this news, I required heavy painkillers and sedatives. I was hysterical. Three days later, Rick and I had to sign the papers to take Jason off life support. The numb feeling I'd known all my life spread out its heavy blanket across my soul, and denial once again became my constant companion as Rick and I flew back to Montana with Jason's body, to prepare for the funeral. I took double and triple doses of any pain medication the doctor would give me. The reality of it all began to creep in when Rick and I were at the funeral home and Jason's body was carried out in a small, white casket.

For years I had not known how to reach the part of myself that would allow me to express the fact that my relationships with men had been chaotic and led to disappointing things. I had been subjected all my life to the raging tirades of an addicted, drunken man. He had died from alcoholism, my husband was an alcoholic, and then my son had died from an alcohol-related accident. Despite any lie I told myself, I was living the legacy of addiction without even knowing it was affecting me until Jason's death. I still didn't see my own addiction, but I definitely knew that Rick's was affecting me in ways I could no longer deny. Living with addiction, up to that point, had actually seemed normal to me because that is all I'd ever known.

A FAMILY HISTORY. OF CRISIS

CHAPTER 2

THE LEGACY OF ADDICTION for Lauren and me began because I was born the daughter of an alcoholic father and she was born the daughter of an alcoholic mom and dad. My father was orphaned as a child and never talked about his past to me. I was told only that things were bad for him. I later found out that his father was also an alcoholic and a very abusive man who abandoned my dad and his siblings, which makes four generations at least of a family nightmare Lauren and I would have to struggle against.

I know little about my grandfather, the person with whom our family legacy of addiction seems to begin, but I do know that he was an only child. His father died when my grandfather was just a baby. As a grown man, he eventually settled in the city of Boston and was heavily involved in bootlegging and prostitution. At some point, that's where he met my grandmother, started a family, and then abandoned them. My grandfather left his wife and all six of his young children to make it on their own, but my grandmother couldn't handle raising this bunch, so she left also. The children were afraid and wanted to stay together after both parents left. They kept their abandonment a secret. My aunt was the oldest of the kids, the rest of whom were boys. She was probably eleven years old when she took on this role; my father was around nine. The youngest child was still just a baby.

My father worked as soon as he was able, taking his red wagon door to door collecting laundry to wash so that he and his siblings had money to buy food. I can't even imagine the fear and frustration a group of abandoned children like that must have felt trying to care for each other at such young ages. It was only discovered that my father and his siblings were living alone when my grandfather's mother went to their home and found the children by themselves. She contacted social services, and the children were taken out of the home. My aunt, my father, and the other kids were placed in an orphanage, The Home for Little Wanderers, which still exists in the city of Boston today.

At the orphanage, all of the kids would be taken to a different church every Sunday, lined up in the back of the church, and made to wait to see if any family in the congregation had an interest in taking one of the children. My uncle tells this story and says the rejection was devastating when they weren't selected. Still, sometimes a family took one of the children in. My father was in and out of multiple foster homes, which leads me to believe that there may have been behavior problems with him. I have heard from family members that he started drinking at a young age. Over the years, he located and reunited with his sister and some of his brothers, and he did eventually find and develop a relationship with both his parents. That's how I know my grandfather died an obese man in a bathtub with a bottle of liquor and a sandwich. I have heard he weighed eight hundred pounds and that it took four policemen to carry his body out of the house after his death.

My father and mother met when he was twenty-three and she was nineteen years old. My mom's father disapproved of my dad. Her father was concerned that his daughter was going to marry a man they knew so little about. My aunt tells me that he asked my father, "Who are your parents? You get your family together and then you can marry my daughter!" That was the catalyst that motivated my father to locate his parents and siblings. After he did, my mother and father were married in a big church ceremony. My dad's parents were able to attend the wedding, because they had been tracked down and reintroduced into his life, but when they entered back into the picture they brought the family addictions with them. My bootlegging grandfather left his bottle of whiskey under the bed when he stayed for the wedding at my mom's house, where her father found the bottle.

The United States had just entered World War II when my parents were married. They dated only a few months because of the war. My father was due to be sent overseas. Their newlywed months were spent at an army base in Alabama, where my dad was preparing to be shipped out. I have letters that my mother wrote to her sister during this time about the pending deployment, saying to her that his "orders were coming through, and they weren't so awfully good." My mom went back home to Connecticut to be with her family once my dad left for the war. She was pregnant with their first child, my older sister. She was born during the war, and my father did not see her until she was six months old because he had been stationed in Europe and couldn't return home.

My brother followed along three years later, after my father had returned home from the war. I was born seven years after that, and as the youngest of the three, I was the one who was most spoiled. Our family lived on the same street as my mother's relatives, which included my aunts, uncles, cousins, and grandmother. It was great having family so close, and I was a very happy child with the exception of my father's temper, drunken nights, and slurring words. It seemed that he was always giving my brother and sister a hard time, but it didn't really affect me. I have heard that my father was physically violent toward my sister and brother when they were young, but that stopped before I was born. He hit me the one time only when I was in high school and got caught drinking, but my sister remembers a time he hit her when she was ten years old. He took a belt to her and beat her severely. The next day she planned to tell her teacher at school but got scared and decided not to, because she was afraid that not only would my father be in trouble but that it might also affect my mother.

I don't remember my dad being home a lot. I think there were many nights he stopped off at the bar for a quick drink and never quite made it out the door, back to us. He was a sporting goods salesman and worked for my uncle, traveling to colleges throughout Connecticut and Massachusetts. He was very good at this work. He used Saturday mornings to do his paperwork, and many Saturday afternoons were then freed up for him to spend drinking and gambling. My father was a high-energy guy who was not only a big drinker but also a high roller who liked to play craps for the chance of making money on the rolls of the dice.

In one of the genealogy searches I have done on my family, I located a newspaper article from 1953 in which the details of a car chase were recounted, describing the way my dad and his friend chased down a man at high speed after he lifted nine hundred dollars off them in a game of craps. My father had been cheated out of his lucky chances because the man was throwing with loaded dice. I was stunned by the amount of money that had been lost, because nine hundred dollars was a small fortune in those days. We were a middle class family and had nice things, but we were not well off enough for my father to be risking that kind of money. He was just that kind of man, though, a big presence. He was an outgoing individual who was the president of several local organizations. When my dad walked into the bar, everyone knew he was there. He was very charming and had a way with people. My father never entered a room; he owned it. His drink was whiskey. He would order a shot and a beer each time he pulled up to the local bar for his almost daily fix. He would down the shot in one gulp and chase it with the glass of beer. It's called a boilermaker, to drink the two like this.

My mother was a sweet, personable woman who was loved by everyone, too. She was quite beautiful and had her share of suitors when she was young, but when she met my dad she was swept off her feet. She was always willing to lend a helping hand to anyone who needed help, like the time when we were driving home and my mother saw a very pregnant neighbor woman hanging clothes out to dry. We stopped our car, and my mother got out and finished the job for our neighbor. People never forgot the little things like this that my mom did for them that they found so meaningful.

The house we lived in was a two-story home that was owned by my mother's older brother. He lived upstairs with my aunt and three older cousins. I have heard he wanted to keep my mother close, to keep an eye on things. I just knew it felt ideal to grow up surrounded by family. Our home was well-decorated, very cozy, and always spotlessly clean. As children, we were all very well-groomed and received the best education possible. From the outside, everything looked good. We never talked about the problems that happened in our home, not even with each other. I learned early on how to act normal even when crazy things were happening.

My mother was the rock in our household. She provided my sense of security. She was very close to her family, and they were often not very pleased with the way my father acted, and how his behavior affected us. When he wasn't home, life was great, and it almost seemed as if we had a normal family. My brother remembers hearing the car pull into the driveway in the evenings, when my father would return, and thinking, "Oh, no!" He says he felt a knot in his stomach, never knowing what frame of mind our father would be in as he walked through our door.

Dinnertime could be very contentious if he was in a bad mood. I ate as fast as I could so that I could get out to play with cousins and neighborhood friends. I became quite the little escape artist. I felt as if I danced around the fringes of my family when my dad was around, and it worked well for me. I once had to sit with my father when my mother went to visit a friend who had taken ill. He drove my mother and me over to her friend's house. When we arrived in their driveway, she started to get out of the car and told me to stay with my father. I panicked. I begged her to let me go with her. She firmly said no and left, and I tried to hold back the tears, but I couldn't stop them from coming. I was terrified to be alone with my father. He told me to stop crying, but the more he yelled, the harder I cried. I was hysterical by the time my mom returned to the car. Little did I know at the time that this was just a glimpse of how my future would play out after she died and my father and I were the only two left in the house.

The stress of dealing with my father also drained my mom. One night, when I was eight years old, my mother had to put out a fire he had caused in their room after coming home drunk and smoking in bed. The mattress caught fire. I woke up, hearing my mother's screams. I smelled smoke and ran out the front door barefoot in my pajamas. A neighbor couple was out for a late night stroll and I told them that our house was on fire. The next thing I knew, there were sirens and fire trucks roaring down our street. My mother doused the fire with water and was able to put it out, but my father had climbed back into the bed in his drunken state, even though it was still in flames. When my uncle came downstairs to help, my mother was sitting at the kitchen table with tears streaming down her face. She said, "I can't take any more; I have got to leave!"

My sister has shared with me that when she was five years old, my mother made a suicide attempt. She had been taking diet pills, and it all ended up with my mother sticking her head inside the oven and turning on the gas. She had to go away to a hospital for several weeks of treatment after the attempt.

It is obvious to me as I look back that the main way my mother tried to help our household cope with the effects of my father's alcoholism was through food. She was a wonderful cook, and the aroma of foods cooking and baking always filled the house. We had three healthy meals a day, but that was not the issue. We engaged in a free-for-all with the food each day by midafternoon. My mother encouraged and subsidized trips to the corner store for candy and other treats. In the evenings, we snacked and watched television. I think it is interesting that the eating started in the afternoon, shortly before my father was due home from work, and continued on through the evening after he arrived home.

My life seemed normal and comfortable in its own strange way, despite all of this. There were a few awful fights I remember my parents having, and I knew that my mom was sad sometimes due to the chaos my father would cause when he was drunk. He didn't come home for dinner many nights, and when he did, he would sometimes get mad at my brother or sister for something they had done. I remember my sister as being a good girl who rarely did anything wrong, yet she claims my father made up things she was guilty of just so he could rage at her. My brother was also a good kid. He got into some trouble here and there but nothing that deserved the tirades of my father. I had come to accept that his chaos was a normal state of living. It was all I had ever known.

There was a heavy air of impending doom that started hanging around our home after I heard the words "breast cancer," "double mastectomy," "chemotherapy," "radiation treatments," and "brain tumor." No one talked to me about what was going on with my mother after it was discovered she had cancer, and I was too afraid to ask. My sister tells of a really bad fight that happened prior to my mom getting sick, during which my dad shoved my mother hard and she fell and hit her breast. She had been hurt very badly and was black and blue for a long time afterward. Several family members blamed my father for her cancer because that was the breast that the first tumor developed in. My sister got married and moved away and my brother went into the Air Force during the time my mother's cancer progressed. I remember the day that things took a bad turn. That was the day the ambulance came for my mom.

My father had driven to work that morning and called the house to check in with my sister, who was staying with us to help care for my mother. She told him that my mom was doing very poorly and that he needed to return home. In his desperation, my father got back in the car but drove the opposite direction from where we lived. By the time he stopped the car, my dad was in Boston, sitting in front of his brother's house, a two-hour drive away. My uncle sat him down and told him firmly that he needed to turn around and go home because his family needed him. Before he could reach home, the ambulance had come for my mother.

I remember standing there watching silently as she was being loaded onto the stretcher. I knew it would be the last time I would ever see her. I felt terrified as I silently watched her being taken away. I wondered what would become of me and my mother. I did not get to say goodbye. I was lying in my bed that night, unable to sleep, when I heard my father burst through the door crying, telling my sister that it was all over. My mom had died alone.

I felt frozen in my bed, with my heart and head racing, not knowing what I was supposed to do. The next day, family members were in and out of the house as arrangements were being made for the funeral. Everyone worried about me because I was showing no emotion. The next night, I slept across the street at my cousin's house. In the middle of the night I was awakened by a shadow in the dark bedroom, which was dressed in a full uniform. It was my brother. He had wanted to see me when he arrived home from the Air Force for the funeral. After he left, I crawled as far under the covers as I could get, and it was my aunt who later found me, sobbing alone in my grief and fear.

I didn't understand what was going on inside of me. I didn't want anyone asking me any questions about it, either. I was playing out the behavior I had learned growing up in my family, to push feelings back until I was numb. At first my mother's death seemed surreal. Other times I felt guilty, wondering what I had done wrong so that God decided to do that to me. I was so confused. My mother's funeral was a blur. The large church was filled to bursting, and there was not a seat to be had. As we were leaving the cemetery, my grieving grandmother grabbed me and led me to the casket. She tore a flower off the casket and gave it to me. I took it, hoping no one had noticed, because I just wanted to disappear.

I was eleven years old when my mother died. I was left alone with my father, and I truly don't think he had a clue what to do with me. I was sent away during the first summer after my mother's death to stay with relatives, where I overheard many discussions about my future. They spoke about where I would live and who would take care of me. I ended up staying with my father in the end. Unfortunately, he was an emotionally immature and angry man. He had no idea how to communicate with an eleven-year-old child. My father had rarely done any parenting while I was growing up, always on the outside of our inner family circle. Sometimes, I wonder if it might have been so difficult for my dad to take care of me because of his own abandonment. Nobody cared for him when he was left in the situation I was left in following my mother's death. Perhaps he didn't know how to go back to that place in his life.

The only thing we had in common was the fact that we were both devastated by the death of my mother. My dad coped by getting drunk and yelling. I pulled within myself to cope. Since my dad rarely made it home after work because of his drinking habit, I spent a lot of time alone in the house, in my room vacillating between sadness, loneliness, and fear, never knowing if or when my father would show up and start screaming at me. What had once been a home filled with a vibrant family now felt like an empty shell. My mom's family had distanced themselves from us by then, due to their own grief, and I felt so isolated by this distance. That's when the addictions began. I recall starting to eat when I wasn't hungry to try and feel better, which seemed to numb the pain. The legacy of addiction that had belonged to my father and grandfather was becoming my beast, too. I blocked out a lot of what happened during those years, but no matter what I did, I couldn't get away from feelings of shame.

My father constantly raged at me. I remember one night he came home and got me out of bed on a school night, at two in the morning. He was angry because the medicine chest in the bathroom where I kept my makeup was too messy. He threw all of my makeup away and made me sit at the kitchen table with him, where he screamed at me and would not allow me to speak. He told me I was a slut because I wore makeup. He told me that I was worthless and would never amount to anything. My dad pounded his fists on the table and said that my mother would be sick if she could see what a mess I had turned out to be. None of his kids had gotten a higher education, he told me, and by God I was going to be the one to go to college. The things he screamed at me were full of contradictions. My father yelled for several hours that night, repeating the same issues while I sat silently in a chair.

If I started to speak during his rages, my dad would scream at me to shut up. My father was a master at using my shame to punish and control me. The result was that I ended up feeling guilty about everything, including my own existence. I let the family illness of addiction consume me to escape the shame I felt heaped upon me by my dad, and just to escape from myself. I was ashamed of who I was. These outbursts happened often with my father. I remember fluctuating during them from feeling afraid to feeling hurt to feeling giddy, like I was floating around the room, and sometimes I just wanted to laugh out loud because it all seemed so ridiculous. I had to control myself, though, no matter what I felt, because I would have really gotten it if I showed my emotions to my dad.

I saved my sorrow for school, where I remember I would make my way through the hallways on days following my father's rages, dragging around so much shame, guilt, hurt, and fear that I felt like a walking, open sore. My father never let my wounds heal. At the time I did not realize that this was what I could expect out of life as the years would go by, and I would marry a chaotic man who also opened the wounds I nursed and caused them to fester. The only time I can remember feeling any type of hope or peace was when I would go and sit in church sometimes by myself. I felt comforted in church, thinking that somehow, someway, things were going to work out. Then I would return home, and that hope would vanish.

I came home to find every kind of explosion you can imagine over the years, like the time I walked into my room and found my dresser drawers dumped out on the middle of the floor. My father had been going through them, had decided they were too messy, and had dumped them out to punish me. I have no idea what he was looking for or why he did it. I never knew what was going to happen next with my dad. I felt like I was betting like he used to on the odds that he would roll a good pair of dice, but it rarely happened, if ever.

What I began to understand about the stories of my father and my grandfather is that their stories were about detachment.

Each man detached from his emotions by using alcohol to numb the pain caused by living. By the time their beast found me, I had also detached from my life. Everything in my world just seemed to be happening somewhere outside of myself, which is why I was able to overlook the effects of my addiction for so long, even after Jason's death. I spent months recovering from this, even healing from my own physical injuries caused by Rick's crash. I resorted to pilfering though people's medicine cabinets after the doctor would no longer prescribe pain medication or tranquilizers for my hysteria, and I stole pain pills as often as I could find them. Rick's drinking and pot smoking escalated at this time, and our lives spun more and more out of control.

We grieved in very different ways for Jason. Rick was extremely emotional about the death and blamed himself. I was stuck in denial and didn't want to talk about it. I turned to school. I threw myself into accounting studies and graduated with a 3.6 grade point average, though my marriage by this time was unraveling rapidly due to addiction, denial, guilt, and stress. Rick became romantically interested in a young girl. This was the knockout punch for me. She called me to say that my husband was in love with her, and that I deserved better. I couldn't believe what I was hearing.

I never recovered from this blow to the marriage. I asked Rick to leave the house, which he did, and I knew the marriage was over. The day after Rick left, I discovered I was pregnant again. I reversed my decision and took him back, deciding to give the marriage one more chance because I didn't believe I could make it without him, not with Lauren and my son, Ryan, on the way. I was scared, exhausted, and overwhelmed. Shortly after Ryan's birth, Rick took a job in Arizona, and I hoped this would be a fresh start. We continued on for a few years together, but the marriage could not survive. It was extremely chaotic when we separated. Rick got heavily into meth use, which caused me to live in fear and anxiety over what he would try to do next. Before the divorce was over, Rick repeatedly threatened me, slashed my tires, stole my car, and beat me up.

I didn't feel the weight of the disappointing circumstances I had created for myself until so many of them were heaped upon me at once. I had truly developed an emotional numbness that was a coping mechanism. To the outside world, I suppose I came across as insensitive because of this detachment, but dealing with real life and real emotions was just too painful an activity. The only way I could be happy was to self-medicate, so that is what I did. In recovery work for this habit, as an adult, I began to put the stories of my father and grandfather together with my behaviors. Growing up affected by their alcoholism molded my character in their likenesses and also taught me to make the decision they had both made to deny the sensation of pain.

I hated that my father was an alcoholic, yet I also chose to abuse alcohol and drugs. Minutes after high school graduation, I bolted from his house, yet I also chose to be involved in a lifestyle that created relationship problems because of the other addicted people in my world. I felt a huge wave of shame and humiliation when I began to see these parallels between my father, my grandfather, and me. How could I have made so many destructive choices? I had just wanted to feel better, like they had, and yet I had played a role in the wrecking of my relationships, just like they had. Maybe, I sometimes still think, had I not been drinking that day, Jason would be alive. Perhaps my dad thought the exact same thing about my mom, believing that had he been there she might have hung on a little bit more.

The legacy of addiction that I inherited from my father and grandfather was also repeated on Rick's side of the family. Although I never saw his parents drink, I knew that both of his grandfathers had drinking problems, and one of them had owned a bar. It seemed that the disease had skipped a generation and now grew in Rick, which led him to make destructive choices when it came to the kids and me. After we divorced, he constantly put them in danger. One weekend, when Lauren and Ryan were visiting with their dad, I got a call from Lauren. It was a Sunday afternoon, and she said I needed to come pick them up because Rick was passed out. They could not wake him up and didn't know what to do. At the time, Lauren was eight. Ryan was six years old. "My God," I thought, "these are babies. What the heck was he thinking?"

I was frustrated and upset as I made the drive to deal with the situation. This type of thing became a pattern, and I became concerned about what the children were being exposed to. I had hit rock bottom with the addiction and insanity in our family when I was with Rick, and when I was thirty I decided to return to church, where I began to realize that I was screwed up and it was time to get help. Because I seldom experienced acceptable behavior growing up, I thought unacceptable behavior was normal, which led to chaos and confusion in my life and relationships. In my initial recovery work, I sought help around the issues I faced as a result of having grown up in an alcoholic home. Early on I recognized how destructive the consequences of addiction were on the kids when they spent time with their dad, and I knew that my recovery was a critical factor for us in my attempt to create a stable home environment. Although I made the decision then to stop using illegal drugs, it would be twelve more years before I would fully realize the extent of my own addiction and become totally sober.

Rick and I had a joint custody agreement where I provided the primary residence, so it wasn't a choice of whether or not they saw their dad. Rick got to have them every other weekend and for six weeks during the summer. Lauren and Ryan didn't disclose much about what went on when they were with Rick unless they had to, and there were many things I wouldn't learn about until much later, which only served to substantiate my fears. At the time, I was afraid for their safety every time they were with Rick. Being the custodial single parent carried a lot of responsibility. I needed Rick's help, and I remember thinking that it just seemed so unfair that I couldn't rely on him. Between his beast of addiction, my need to work to support the kids, and the decisions I had made to work on my own recovery through meetings, I was overwhelmed and exhausted by the time I had to face the disappointments I had created.

Then, there were the letters to Lauren and Ryan that arrived from Rick through the years. These were postmarked from various jails and prisons where he had been sentenced, due to arrests for driving under the influence. My heart would break for my children as each letter arrived for them. The legacy of addiction continued for us all in these notes, in which Rick repeated promises I knew he could not keep, like that he was truly going to be there for the kids and make up for the times he had let them down. The sad thing is that I think he meant every word he said. He just couldn't deliver.

The exposure of the kids to our family story of addiction only increased after Rick married his third wife, Sylvia, with whom he opened a new chapter in the book. She was violent to the children. Lauren was twelve and Ryan ten years old when I had to come and rescue them from her abuse. About three weeks into the summer I received a panicked phone call from Lauren, claiming Sylvia had gotten physical with them. They had escaped the apartment but needed me to come and pick them up. On the forty-mile drive to rescue my kids, I was practically hyperventilating. When I arrived, Rick was standing in front of the apartment complex where he and Sylvia lived, and though Lauren and Ryan were there, too, all Rick could say was that he didn't really know what was going on. He just shrugged his shoulders, walked off, and shook his head.

The kids told me that Sylvia had kicked Ryan and had thrown him up against a wall. They had told Rick what had happened, but he hadn't believed them. I thought about my father and Nora, and how I would overhear her force my father to say that he loved her more than he loved me. I could never tell my father about the way Nora mistreated me, because I believe he would have sided with her, just like Rick had done with Sylvia, leaving my kids to live my story all over again. The jealousy of the alcoholic, abusive stepmother was playing itself out in yet another generation of our family. I filed a police report against Sylvia, yet I was told that without physical bruises on the children there was not much that the police could do. The police recommended that I file a complaint with Child Protective Services, which I did, but at this point I knew I could not count on Rick to be there consistently for Lauren and Ryan unless I wanted to subject them to more of the same.

I know now that Lauren began smoking cigarettes shortly after her dad disappeared from her life. She became an angry young preteen. I had bought a home in a nicer part of town, an act I was very proud of as a single mother, to have come so far from my own story of addiction. This move caused two major changes for my children. One was that their favorite baby sitter no longer lived next door. The second change was that Lauren and Ryan had to change schools twice during this time, due to a job offer I received in Colorado. I decided to take the job, which caused us all to move a second time after our split from Rick. The first signs of trouble began brewing then. Lauren and Ryan began spending time with new friends, a sister and brother, Christy and Danny, who lived nearby. Not long after, Lauren started talking back to me, doing obvious things to provoke me, and becoming difficult to deal with.

I didn't know it was addiction with her at first. I remember believing it was regular teenager things. Once, she took the dog out for a walk and did not come back until late into the night. When I asked her what had been going on, she screamed at me, "Leave me the hell alone and get out of my face!" Lauren stomped up the stairs and slammed her bedroom door. But around the house, there were other signs. She wasn't doing her chores, and when I would confront her about this, she would give me nasty remarks and attitude. It wasn't like her to be so angry, so often. I was beginning to wonder what the heck was wrong. I was frustrated, because I really needed her and Ryan to be responsible; I needed their help, and it just wasn't happening. I sometimes wonder if Lauren would not have become totally out of control at this point had I followed my gut and provided constant supervision, but then again I think maybe it wouldn't have mattered. Addiction is powerful when it has been maturing silently in the next generation, especially in a hurting girl like Lauren, or a hurting girl like I had been, years before.

OUR SPIRAL DOWN

CHAPTER 3

I KNEW SOMETHING was off when Lauren's behavior changed.
Still, it was challenging to figure out how to handle this suspicion.
She was too old for a baby sitter by this time, but she did not seem
trustworthy enough to be left alone. I counted on school starting
up again to make her life busy and distracted, and I hoped things
would go back to the way they had been with her when things were
good in Arizona. That was before I had taken the job in Colorado
that moved us away from the friends that each of us had counted
on for support. I couldn't have been more mistaken believing that
distraction can stop an illness that is passed on through the family.
It was about to flare up, not settle down.

Lauren went into ninth grade at a high school near our home. Ryan went into seventh grade that year, at the middle school. He was doing poorly with his grades and started telling me he was sick many mornings and unable to go to school. Too often I let him stay home. I called the house frequently and stopped by to check on him on my lunch hour, but he was already doing drugs by this time and purposely evaded my calls and knew how to avoid me when I came over. Then calls from the vice principal started coming. I started by trying to talk to Ryan about it; then I yelled at him, grounded him, and even dragged him to school on days he wasn't supposed to be staying home. I felt powerless.

I couldn't make a consistent change in Ryan, so I sought help and finally took him to a psychologist. From there we were referred to a psychiatrist for an evaluation, because it was suspected that a psychological disorder lay at the root of his behaviors. The psychiatrist asked Ryan questions and concluded he had ADHD (attention deficit/hyperactivity disorder). The psychiatrist put Ryan on medication, and I sent him back to school, where his attendance and grades improved considerably. I thought we had solved the problem as quickly as it had flared up. During this lull, Ryan called me up at work to say he had spilled a bunch of his pills into a mess of Kool-Aid, had to throw the pills down the drain, and needed me to get him more drugs. I really didn't realize at the time that this story was a sign. We hadn't scratched the surface of the problem at all.

I had gone ahead and gotten Ryan's prescription refilled because it was one of those stories I just had a funny feeling about but dismissed. It's a fleeting thought that came back to haunt me.

I found out he had been passing his ADHD pills around to friends so they could get high. I didn't listen to my instinct or see my own historical pattern repeating in my kid. I know now that the feeling I had about Ryan's story wasn't odd. The feeling was familiar. I had lived the same story before, passing out pain pills I stole from my dad. I believe I chose denial instead of deciding to look deeper into what was going on with Ryan. I hoped that things would just get better on their own, which is almost always a mistake, because they rarely do and in our case did not. School administrators started calling about Lauren, who was about to take the starring role in our story of addiction.

Her vice principal had let me know she had attitude problems with her teachers. I decided to take her to a psychologist, like I had taken Ryan, to try to get to the root of her problem. The psychologist felt that there was something going on but could not figure it out, though she was concerned enough to recommend Lauren come back and believed maybe then we would get to the bottom of Lauren's behavior. My relationship with Lauren got worse as I took her to these appointments, but we continued going to counseling anyway. That school year, she failed most of her classes. I was concerned, but I didn't press harder to turn her grades around because our family was already going through problems with Ryan, they were both seeing counselors, and I felt overwhelmed. I believed I was doing all I could to deal with the situation. I didn't know what other steps to take.

As I tried to keep us all together, Lauren began to spend more time with Christy, the new friend she had made in our neighborhood. I had mixed feelings about this girl. Christy and her brother, Danny, came as a pair. He had clicked with Ryan while Christy and Lauren hit it off, but I sensed the four of them together could be trouble. During the second semester of school, what I sensed might happen, did. Lauren and Christy got caught smoking and ditching school, and both continued to have attitude problems with their teachers. I tried to talk to Lauren about this, but she was only rude to me. She would deny that she was agitating her teachers. She actually claimed it was they who were out to get her. At home, Lauren began to stay out later than I allowed. If I got upset, she would just start arguing with me. I also started to notice that she had been steadily losing weight.

I should have paid more attention to the weight loss because of the sign it was pointing to. Had I realized that drugs and alcohol were involved, it might have dawned on me that her using had become more important to her than her health. The behavior issues with her, though, were such a distraction that it was all I could do to deal with the daily challenges that were in my face. One night she didn't come home at all, which scared me to death. The possibility that my daughter had been kidnapped, raped, or murdered made me sick to my stomach. I was angry and asked myself what she could have possibly been thinking to do something like that. I had to call the police and file a report. I didn't sleep all night, and in the morning I had to make a difficult call to my boss. My life with the kids had escalated to a point where I could no longer keep hiding. Until Lauren disappeared, I had been able to manage our family without it affecting my work, but after she vanished it pushed the two worlds into collision. My boss had no idea when I told her that I was having trouble with my children.

After I called my boss, I phoned the police again and called the psychologist that Lauren and I had been seeing. She recommended Lauren be hospitalized in an adolescent psychiatric hospital. I was sick with worry, and Lauren was still missing. Only Ryan was able to help me find her in the end, and it turned out she had run away with Christy, so I called her mother and we decided to work together to find the girls. Christy's mom was extremely angry. We joined forces as allies at first, but it wasn't long before she turned against me, blaming Lauren as the troublemaker.

In the meantime I called the hospital. I made arrangements to admit Lauren as soon as I could get her back, but I had concluded by then that the girls were not going to be easy to find. It wasn't going to do me any good to sit home day after day, waiting until Lauren decided to come home. I went back to work, but I felt like an emotional mess trying to function at my job. On day three, I couldn't take it anymore. Christy's mother and I got together again to search for the girls. We went to the house of a girl whom we heard Lauren and Christy had been hanging around with and knocked on the door. Her teenage brother answered and got nasty with us when we asked to come in and look around, which gave me the feeling that something was up. I listened to this feeling, pulled around the corner of the house, and staked it out.

Within twenty minutes, a car pulled into the driveway. Out of the front door of the house bolted our two runaway daughters, hell-bent to enter the waiting car and continue their spree. I am sure they had been told we were close on their heels. I pulled up behind the car after I saw the girls make a run for it, so that the vehicle couldn't back out. Christy's mom jumped out of our car and started screaming at her daughter. The chaos got the attention of the entire neighborhood, which forced us to explain what was going on with our kids. I asked the neighbors to call the police, and within three minutes, a fire truck, an ambulance, and two police cars were on the scene. The girls were released to our custody. I tried to take Lauren to the hospital, just as I had planned, though of course word had gotten back to her, from Ryan, that she was headed for inpatient. Her first words to me when she got in the car were "I am not going to any fucking hospital!"

She demanded that I stop at a gas station so she could use the bathroom. She screamed that she needed a cigarette and told me she wanted me to stop at the store. I had given in so many times in the past when she had demanded and negotiated things, but not this time. I suddenly realized I had turned a corner as I began to drive. My life had been consumed by this obsession over the drama with my children. Although I had made some efforts with counselors for them, I was at a point where I was ready to do whatever it took to get things turned around, no matter how uncomfortable that would make our lives. This was a major breakthrough for me. I kept silent as I drove Lauren straight to the hospital without any stops.

She asked me to please not do it when I began to check her in, but I didn't know what else to do. Lauren needed more help than I could give her. I walked her in, and then she was led away. I left the hospital feeling frozen, yet relieved. The staff had told me to go home and try to get some sleep. This is when I began to connect our story to the legacy of addiction. I came back the next afternoon to meet with the doctor assigned to Lauren, who began to complete a family history chart for us. I noted addictions in the lives of Rick, my father, my grandfather, and myself, and as I talked, the doctor just shook her head and said, "Wow . . . no wonder."

Lauren was brought in the room after that. She was extremely upset, sobbing like a baby, begging that I take her home. It was a welcome change to see her vulnerable, with her walls down. She threw herself on me and told me that she was afraid and that there were some very scary people in that place. Lauren promised that she wouldn't run away again if I would only let her come home. I wanted to believe her, so I asked the psychologist what we should do. She said that taking Lauren home would be a bad idea. It was incredibly hard to tell Lauren that she needed to stay, but I did, and immediately this changed her whole demeanor. She became angry and sullen, the exact same Lauren I was used to seeing at home, which broke my heart.

Before being discharged, Lauren spent one week at this hospital. I felt horrible to have left her in a place that she felt was scary. I felt like a train had run over me. I felt such a burden from the choice I had made, and still I needed to trust the professionals at that time. They recommended Lauren not return to the house after her release, so instead I arranged to have her stay in Montana, with Rick's parents. I still called to discuss the kids with Rick; he went in and out of sobriety, and the responsible phases could sometimes accompany them. After talking the situation through with him, he agreed that sending Lauren to his parents' house was a good option. She had always been very close to her grandparents, and especially her grandmother. They agreed to take her for a few months after we called to let them know.

I picked Lauren up from the hospital when she was discharged, driving her directly to the airport, where I put her on a plane to Montana. She was relieved to be out of the hospital and excited to go to see her grandparents. I was just grateful that she was safe. Lauren did great in Montana as far as I knew, although I wasn't getting the total picture. She didn't want to talk to me when I would call her. She was upset over what I had done. Her grandmother told me this, and she sent photographs of Lauren that were shot by her grandfather. In the photos I could see she had gained some of her weight back and looked really healthy, but Lauren would later tell me she was bored in Montana. I didn't see it. I saw a girl in the pictures who was happier than she had been before, which made me feel so relieved. Ryan was at home during this time. He made it through the rest of the school year with passing grades, and things were fairly quiet at our house until the next school year.

The summer vacation passed more easily than I expected it to. I had been dreading that I would have to plan what to do with both kids, as Lauren would be back from Montana by that time because I couldn't leave her with her grandparents forever. Leaving either of them home alone while I worked, however, was not an option, so I sent them both down to Arizona for summer break. Rick was living there, and the kids spent a good part of that summer with their godmother, Mary. The hope that this quiet summer would somehow last died away as soon as the school year began again, in Colorado. It didn't take long before I was getting phone calls that Lauren had ditched school, was having attitude problems, and was failing her classes, just like before.

I couldn't figure out what was happening to my family that was causing all this chaos. I had tried the steps I knew were supposed to reverse behaviors and control uncontrollable kids. I enforced consequences as best I could, took the kids to doctors, and had used the help of an inpatient hospital to deal with the behavioral issues. None of this had worked. I was missing work often by this time to meet with school officials and counselors on behalf of Lauren or Ryan. I felt helpless. One night in my bedroom, I got on my knees and prayed for knowledge that would help and guide my family. I got my answer the next afternoon. A marijuana pipe was lying on my couch. I kept thinking *I'm shocked!* Even though the kids said the pipe belonged to Christy, clearly I knew that my kids were doing drugs. I felt overwhelmed by disbelief and disappointment. I thought we had gotten away from the addicts in our lives. I had worked so hard to change our circumstances through all of the counseling and recovery work. Creating and maintaining a stable home environment for my children had been my highest priority. Now the disease of addiction was right back in our lives and worse than ever. How could this possibly be happening? I had to wake up to the fact that nothing was out of the range of possibility. Everything I'd refused to believe about Lauren and Ryan's behavior and all the insanity that went along with it was starting to make sense.

I accepted the pipe story that Lauren and Ryan told me, that it belonged to Christy. She played along and said that the pipe was hers. Then she begged me not to tell her mother and said that she knew she needed help. I was easily impressed by these kinds of seemingly honest, heartfelt reactions. Rather than look for the lie in Christy's story, I was hopeful that maybe if my kids could become as honest as she was, there might be progress for us all. The kids strung me along with this hope for a long time. I had taken Christy back to our house on the day I found the pipe to sit her down with Lauren, Ryan, and her brother, Danny, to ask everyone to be honest. I gave Christy and Danny my word I would not tell their parents and shared stories about what happens to kids that get hooked on drugs. I revealed things about my own past drug use and told everyone about the accident that killed Jason. When I thought they were on board, I even said that I planned to use my time to find recovery meetings for them all. I found out much later on that none of them really wanted help. They just wanted to appease me. It amazes me that I was so blind to the lies and manipulation, because I had done some of the same types of things to my dad when I was a teen.

The irony of family addiction is that when you are faced with a loved one's addiction, you go through the typical denial, anxiety, enabling, and fierce need to control that anyone does who is facing the situation for the first time, or has not struggled with addiction personally. I was going to save them all! Not. I was recovered from drugs at the time, but even I was not sober yet from alcohol. I was coming from my level of understanding at the time, which had not progressed to the point where I was able to admit that all of us were addicts: Lauren, Ryan, and me. Lauren and I remained in therapy, and after this pipe incident came out in one of our sessions, the counselor pulled me aside and recommended that I tell Christy and Danny's mom. The counselor told me I really didn't have the right to keep such important information from a parent, no matter what I had previously promised. So I followed through. Once I did, the kids were furious. Christy and Danny no longer trusted me, and Lauren and Ryan were especially angry, which only strengthened the addictive beast in them.

I called my best friend, Shirley, who was back in Phoenix, when this happened, because I hoped she could give me some ideas on where I should go to get help. She told me about the Tough Love program. It helps parents deal with children that have behavior problems. Shirley had been using Tough Love techniques with her daughter, Lindsey, who had experienced similar problems to Lauren's. I started attending weekly Tough Love meetings after I spoke to Shirley, and I learned I did not have to accept unacceptable behavior from my children. I learned techniques to draw boundaries between the kids and myself and how to run the house as a parent, not a friend. Of course, when one person in a family starts to change for the better, everyone else gets crazy. Lauren and Ryan started staying out later on school nights as a way to react to the fact that our system had begun to change, but because the town we lived in had a curfew set for adolescents, I could make calls to the police when they were out past curfew. This floored the kids. They could not believe I would do such an awful thing to them. I became the enemy, and our situation turned into a war.

I had started to feel a little better as I gained the upper hand, sure, but Lauren and Ryan seemed to be getting worse despite the Tough Love techniques. Both children were busted at their schools for drugs. They were failing classes still, ditching school, and often suspended. Neither could do anything without receiving a consequence from me, which gave me the sense I was taking some of my power back, and yet I believe the kids were actually happy each time they were suspended. It allowed them to stay home alone and do what they wanted. It actually felt like more of a punishment for me than for them.

Lauren became a thief during this time to sustain her addictive behaviors. In her room, I found a drawer full of pictures of a family I did not know along with a wallet that belonged to a neighbor. I didn't understand how it had gotten into my daughter's room, because it wasn't my first instinct to believe Lauren was committing crimes. I took the wallet and put it in the neighbor's mailbox without leaving a note or an explanation. The familiar numb feeling from childhood came over me. I remembered that my addiction was no longer mine to control when I began to steal from my father. I was deep in denial that Lauren could have reached this stage. One day shortly after, I went down in the basement and thought I saw a dead body on the couch. I threw the covers back, but underneath there were just some pillows and a wadded-up blanket. It made me realize the level of insanity I was living in that by then I practically expected to discover a dead body in my basement, because I had discovered everything else.

I decided it was time to get specific help for at least Lauren's drug problems, and I called a counseling office that specialized in substance abuse. I started taking her and Ryan to the office every Saturday morning. The counselor spent individual time with me as well. She encouraged me to do new things for myself, like take an exercise class and try to get out of the house more often to socialize with friends. The counselor also told me to try not to be anxious over what I could not control. If I could completely accept my inability to control Lauren and deal with my own fear and controlling impulses instead, I could open myself up to learning positive actions. Regardless of how I might be contributing to problems Lauren had, the choices she was making were 100 percent her own.

It took time before I was ready to embrace this philosophy. After going to the sessions for several months, I began to feel like I was making progress in accepting this fact, but Lauren had continued with business as usual. We seemed to be on opposite paths. Because a change hadn't occurred in her behaviors, our counselor sat me down and told me that she had done as much as she could to help Lauren. The counselor informed me that both of my kids were actively using drugs and were unwilling to change, because they liked their lifestyle too much. She recommended that I hospitalize them for substance abuse, so I called our health insurance company to see if this was possible. The insurance company put me in touch with a local hospital, where I took Lauren and Ryan to be evaluated on the same day I called.

The drive seemed like an eternity, as the kids sat sullenly in the back seat. The hospital decided that Lauren and Ryan should both be admitted into the day treatment program. I was to drop them off daily, at nine, and return to pick them up at four in the afternoon, Monday through Friday for six weeks. This was terrible for me because of my work schedule. The hospital was a forty-five-minute drive from our house, which meant I had to tell my boss that I needed a leave of absence or to work only partial days. Still sympathetic to my situation, my boss told me to come in late every morning and leave early if I needed to. She said not to worry about taking a leave, but even with this flexibility, it was a rough six weeks. The most frustrating thing was the fact that in the hospital nobody was able to control Lauren or Ryan better than I had.

Lauren was caught smoking during her first week of the program, and then she admitted to smoking pot in the mornings before we left the house each day during week two. Ryan fared only slightly better, because he was diagnosed with signs of depression and put on new medication. We had believed he was suffering from ADHD, but this change in his evaluation led to a new prescription drug. I went along with it, although I was unsure at the time because our previous doctor had been so adamant regarding Ryan's ADHD diagnosis. I remembered that when I felt depressed at his age, I had used marijuana, and I wondered if Ryan's issue might be similar. I began to wonder if any of these professionals actually knew what they were really dealing with.

This was another of the periods when Rick was doing well enough to be in communication with the kids. I contacted him about the situation, and he decided it was time for him to make a surprise visit. Rick had been released from prison, was sober, and had separated from Sylvia because she had continued to drink during his recovery. The look on the faces of our kids was priceless when their dad walked through the door. At first, Lauren had a look of excitement, but she caught herself after she realized this visit was not for fun. She sat down with Rick, Ryan, and me, and as parents we told them that we were no longer going to accept their behavior. I told them that if they did not straighten up, we were moving from Colorado back to Arizona, close to Rick, where we at least had support.

Lauren and Ryan listened attentively, not happy with what Rick and I had said. It was beginning to get tougher for the kids to enjoy their lifestyles of addiction, which was a change I wanted to make after our counselor had said the enjoyable way of life I had allowed was part of our problem. The week after Rick left, I got a phone call from the hospital. Lauren was trying to enjoy her addicted lifestyle in the hospital instead. There had been some hysteria because a few patients had taken hits of hallucinogenic LSD. Lauren was the one responsible for bringing the drugs to the program.

I had no idea she had been smuggling in drugs. It went back to the fact that I had been letting go of my control issues, because there was no way I could have searched Lauren's clothing, backpack, body, and purse every day. If she wanted drugs that badly, she was going to find a way to outsmart me, yet the hospital was up in arms and wanted to throw her out. Why was the counselor so surprised that Lauren was acting the exact same way at the program as she acted at home? Why did the counselor think I had brought her there for treatment in the first place? I wanted the counselor to be able to control the problems I couldn't, and here I was listening to the staff at the hospital complaining about their inability to change Lauren's behavior. Weren't these the experts?

I expressed my outrage, and the counselor backed down from

threatening to kick Lauren out. They started coming down hard on her with consequences instead. She was switched from the outpatient facilities to inpatient for a day and forced to spend the night in the program, as one punishment. She had been caught bringing in someone else's urine for her drug test. I later found out the urine she had taken belonged to a neighborhood girlfriend of Lauren's who had been in trouble with the law and had urine to share because she was required to supply it for weekly drug tests.

It seemed logical to me that if Lauren needed to be monitored constantly to catch all her tricks, perhaps the professionals should have recommended inpatient treatment. Nobody ever did. The hospital actually encouraged me to give Lauren some freedom and allow her to occasionally see friends. I was at the end of my rope. I felt overwhelmed, hopeless, angry, and discouraged. Though I had threatened Lauren and Ryan with the possibility that we would move back to Arizona, it wasn't what I wanted, and yet a series of things led straight there. I found out that a large Canadian corporation was purchasing the company I worked for, and my department of two was to be downsized. I opted to take the severance package the company offered me. Afterward, I sent out job applications and within a week had two positions offered to me in Phoenix. I had enough money saved by that time to purchase a home if I took either job, so Lauren, Ryan, and I moved a third time.

The home I bought in Phoenix was close to the church we had attended the last time we had lived in Arizona, and it was located only two miles from my friend Shirley's home. Shirley and her daughter, Lindsey, were still having issues at that time, but things had improved since she had learned the Tough Love techniques and applied them in their home. My kids had not improved in the least. Before we left Colorado, Lauren stole some of my checks in the hope she could run away again, rather than move; however, she did not follow through. Ryan was adamant that he was not going to live with me and decided to go live with his dad, in Cottonwood, Arizona, a two-hour drive from the house where Lauren and I ended up. It upset me, but I let Ryan make his own decision. He wouldn't be that far away, and he would come home to spend the weekend a couple of times per month.

I continued to attend Tough Love meetings in Phoenix, with Shirley, and made sure there were consequences for any unacceptable behaviors Lauren tried to pull. As I settled in with her, things were less chaotic than they had been in Colorado. She even seemed to become inspired. She asked to go to a new, charter high school where the courses were designed to let her work at her own pace. Lauren actually went to school most of the time after I said yes and enrolled her, and she also got a job at a telemarketing company. I was pleased she was making progress in her life. Both the kids, in fact, seemed renewed. Perhaps it was due to the surprise they felt when I actually followed through with the threat of the move. In any event, this was a period when things were fairly peaceful, and I welcomed the needed break. Lauren was keeping from me what was just around the bend for her.

FALSE HOPE

LAUREN TURNED SIXTEEN the year we moved back to Arizona, and she resumed old friendships. I was so relieved. She had been close to her friend Steve since they were three years old. He was a good kid, and I couldn't have been more pleased when Lauren contacted him. She also spent time with Shirley's daughter, Lindsey, whom she had known for a number of years. I was a bit concerned about Lauren's involvement with Lindsey, because she had caused Shirley so much trouble, but the girls had known each other for a long time. Might they be good for each other? Shirley's advice had certainly been good for me. Lauren also met Robert, her boyfriend at the time, shortly after we moved. He was a nineteen-year-old she had been introduced to through her godmother Mary's family. Robert seemed like a nice kid and had known Mary's family for years, although I remember thinking he did not seem like Lauren's type. I didn't understand what she saw in him.

Halfway through the semester Ryan attempted to move home, but that move was put on hold. I called Rick, and we decided it was better for Ryan to finish the school year first. At the time I was unaware, but found out later on, that Rick had relapsed. I had wondered what was up when Ryan wanted to come home. Turns out, Rick was drinking pretty heavily and so was his wife, and things were rocky in their marriage. It's distressing to think Ryan had to tolerate the same type of environment I did, when my dad married Nora and they were both drinking a lot. He still came home on weekends, and when he did, Lauren, Ryan, and I started going back to our old church together. It was comforting to once again walk through the doors of the sanctuary, where so much healing had occurred for me.

I was where I belonged, but Lauren was not. She was still trying to figure out if she belonged to herself or to her addictions. I had high hopes. Our church had one of the biggest teen programs in the country, and I had told Lauren that if she went on a retreat, I would pay to get her driver's permit. She looked angry at first that she had to participate to get the privilege she wanted, but she quickly reconsidered her response and said okay. That spring she attended the teen retreat, with over one hundred other teens. When she came back she was quiet and looked angry. It wasn't quite what I had hoped for, and I wasn't sure how to read her. My initial take was that she must not have liked the retreat. Perhaps she was irritated with me for having forced the issue. What I found out years later was that she had a wonderful, spiritual weekend. Lauren had made the decision to stop using drugs, which had been an overwhelming release.

At the time Lauren came home, I had no idea what she was thinking. She seemed so withdrawn. But soon after, Lauren started looking forward to going to church on Sunday and agreed to attend the eight-month-long confirmation program at our church. The problem was that her addiction had progressed too far by this point. Although she had decided she did not want to belong to her addiction any longer, there was no way Lauren could stop with just one promise at a weekend retreat. I certainly remember being at that point, when I believed I could quit using drugs on my own. It was shortly after my divorce, and probably a few months after I had started attending church. I had gone out with a friend to play pool and drink a few beers, and that night my friend ran into someone who had some cocaine, and the next thing I knew I was snorting lines with her in the bathroom of the pool hall. I couldn't understand how I could let myself down after I had decided to never do drugs again. Lauren wouldn't be able to follow through either. It feels like you can reclaim your life when you promise to quit using, but you can't, not without a bigger change.

That summer was fairly quiet for us. We had no major incidents that I can recall. When school started in September, Ryan was living back home, just as I had promised, and Lauren was back at the charter school. It wasn't long after that that I began receiving the same calls I always did. Ryan wasn't showing up for school. Lauren had started to break curfew, skip school and work, and spend most of her time with her boyfriend, Robert. I got fed up with it all one day and told the children that I wasn't going to accept the rule breaking and that if it continued, the consequences would come. I began by removing every TV and radio from the house. I drove them all over to Shirley's house, to store in her garage. I couldn't lift the big TV, so I simply cut the cord with a pair of scissors.

After I started Tough Love, I had consistently issued consequences, and yet somehow Lauren and Ryan remained in disbelief that I would follow through. It was actually part of a cycle I didn't see. After my consequences, the kids seemed to settle down. Then because of the improved behavior I would loosen up the reins, and they would take to their old behaviors again, and we were back at the start. It was a wild balancing act in those days. I had parenting, work, church, recovery meetings, and life in general to contend with. It was during this time that I met Bob, my current husband. We met at work and started dating, but out of embarrassment for my situation I didn't initially volunteer any information about the problems with Lauren and Ryan. As Bob and I got more serious, I told him what had been going on. I was surprised and relieved when Bob said he supported me and would help me in any way that he could. He seemed like a nice, normal, down-to-earth guy. It was good timing for me to meet a man like that, because I had stayed out of relationships while I worked on my recovery issues. I had reached a point where I was ready to date, trusted myself to make better choices, and knew I could use all the help I could get.

The kids and I went to Florida that year, to my sister's house for Thanksgiving, and our problems from home followed us there. Money began disappearing from the purses and wallets of family members. My brother-in-law pulled me aside and told me about the thefts. I couldn't imagine who would do something like that, because despite all the proof otherwise, as a mother I still refused to imagine that I had raised bad kids. "Please," I thought to myself, "don't let it be my children," but of course it had been. My brother-in-law had set a trap by putting a wallet on the dining room table and setting up a video camera, and it was Ryan who was caught on tape. Thanksgiving morning my brother-in-law confronted him, but Ryan denied it, and then on the day we left for the airport, my brother-in-law came running out of the house and grabbed Ryan again. What now?

"Where is it?!" my brother-in-law screamed. "Where's the gun!" I was stunned when I heard the word "gun." I thought this was still about the wallet, but it was not. Things had gone almost as far as the possibility of the dead person in my basement. My brother-in-law informed me that someone had taken a loaded pistol out of a hidden place in the house. At this point my sister grabbed Ryan's suitcase and began to go through it. "Nothing here," she called. She yanked Lauren's suitcase out and started going through it as well. Sure enough, there was the gun. Ryan had secretly hidden it. Lauren's eyes got wide when she saw it, and her mouth dropped in shock.

Lauren firmly stated that she had nothing to do with the gun. My brother-in-law was screaming at Ryan by this time, which caused him to run off crying into the woods behind their home. We were already late for the airport as Ryan tore off into the forest. We all yelled for him, but he would not answer, and the woods behind my sister's home were thick, so it was unlikely he could hear our calls. My sister took charge. "You have to get on that plane because you have to go to work tomorrow." She told me that she and my brother-in-law would find Ryan. I followed her advice, boarded the plane, and was overwhelmed with feelings by the time I reached Bob at the other end.

I had gotten on a plane without my fourteen-year-old son, who was lost in the woods in Florida and had just stolen a gun. I called my sister a couple of times in flight but there had been no sign of Ryan. Lauren and I were both upset and talked about our fears during the flight, which created a bond between us that felt real. What if they didn't find him? we wondered. What if he got so lost in those dense woods that he couldn't find a way out? What were we going to say to Bob? We were both in the same shoes, feeling traumatized, affected by the addiction of someone that we loved. When Bob saw this on my face and noticed I was missing one child, he sat me down. He had been waiting with flowers in hand when Lauren and I landed. This is when I told him everything. If we needed to, he said, we could catch a flight back and find Ryan.

We called my sister again before making a choice. When I reached her, she informed me Ryan had been found. He was huddled in a corner on her back porch. She had found him sleeping, curled up with the dog. She was going to let him sleep it off and get him a flight out to Arizona the next day. I can imagine he was frightened to death in those woods, and even more scared when he came out to learn that his mother and sister had got on a plane and left him, thousands of miles away. I believed this was for the best, and that it was a powerful, natural consequence for Ryan. Once I got over being worried, I also felt justified. I was forced into the choice to a degree, and I had been angry, but it was necessary. My son had stolen money and a gun and had dragged the entire family into his mess.

I called the psychiatrist who had prescribed Ryan's depression medication, and when Ryan returned to Arizona we went in and talked to her. She recommended that we speak with a substance abuse specialist. Ryan met with this person, who then asked me to step into his office to discuss what he had learned. The specialist told me Ryan had no interest in stopping his drug use. There was a program, but the specialist suggested that I not bother because it wouldn't do any good given my son's attitude. I couldn't believe the discouraging news. If there was no hope, what was left? At this point I was also dealing with another school situation. Ryan and another boy, Justin, had both been found in possession of drugs. Ryan had LSD in his pocket and a marijuana pipe. The police were brought in, and Ryan was suspended indefinitely.

I refused to function without hope. I was not ready to concede defeat, and I decided that if I had to fight to get my kids help, then so be it. I contacted the psychologist who had said Ryan wasn't ready to get help for his drug problem, and I pushed to get my son into the substance abuse program anyway. It was a six-week program in which kids met three nights per week in the evenings, reserving Wednesday nights for treatment that included the whole family. This meant Lauren, too, which was essential, because as a unit our family had become an unmanageable force. These family sessions were intense and confrontational. Most kids we met in the program had been court-ordered to attend. None of the kids attending appeared to like the program, and the parents just seemed overwhelmed and depressed. I was uncomfortable. At some of the sessions, things got heated between parents and their kids.

It almost felt as if the families were being humiliated in front of everyone. There is an intense shame and embarrassment about addiction. Allowing others to look at your life makes you vulnerable. Addiction makes you feel like such a mess, that you should have been smarter, and you can't believe how enormous you have allowed the beast of addiction to grow. Five weeks into this process, Ryan's weekly drug test came up clean for the first time. Everyone clapped, and he looked proud. What I didn't know was that he went out that night and got high to celebrate. He had no desire to stop using drugs, but I was happy in a deluded bliss that he was finally sober, and I thought that Lauren might learn a thing or two from him. Ryan just went along for the ride to appease me, which made the celebrations we shared with the other families in our adolescent drug group a kind of false hope. The real hope was in remaining vigilant for my children. When Ryan graduated from the drug group, I asked to know more about a twelve-step program I heard about. Attending weekly meetings was one of the conditions of his release.

The other kids in his adolescent drug group badmouthed the

twelve-step program. They said it was a cult. This was because in the twelve-step program addicts weren't allowed any slack. They were out if they continued to use drugs. One mother pulled me aside to confirm that in the program her son had been sober and done fantastically when he had been attending. It was only his own choice to leave, to go back to using, which had caused him to end up in the adolescent drug group for teens. The twelve-step group was for kids who wanted to get sober permanently and learn to live a happy life. At previous counseling and programs, Lauren and Ryan were told that they had better change or else terrible things would happen, but they were never given any solutions as to how they might make changes. In contrast, the twelve-step program was supposed to teach them how to get and stay sober. I needed the hope of this promise that my kids could have a great life.

I called the contact number for the twelve-step group and was asked to meet with a parent at a coffee shop, located at the center where the teen group met. I was also interested in asking the parent how to sign Ryan up for the "sober" school I had heard about, which many of the kids involved in the twelve-step program were attending. Bob and I arrived early at the coffee shop. It was located in a large outside mall area. Soon after we got there, kids and parents began showing up at the coffee shop all around us, and the energy level of these kids left me stunned. The young people ranged in age from thirteen to seventeen years old. They were laughing and happy and playing around, having the time of their lives, something Lauren would be taken by later. These kids had the energy she remembered herself having, before her addictions had caused her to become a withdrawn shell of her former self.

There was a group of teens playing red rover near us. Another group was at a table playing cards, and both groups had kids that were laughing and whooping and jumping up and down. Some teens counseled others, just trying to help them out. The most amazing thing was that all of them were interacting with their parents in positive ways. The energy in the air was electric, alive, and full of life. I had to hold back the tears as my emotions overwhelmed me. I felt as if I had been on a long hard journey and had finally found a home. I didn't know what I had just experienced, but I knew deep down that my life was about to change. For the first time in years, I felt the sense of hope I had known I needed, which was different from the desperate type of hope I would have each time a new start with Lauren or Ryan seemed promising. Something was obviously working there, as was evident by the smiling parents and their enthusiastic daughters and sons.

The parent Bob and I had arranged to meet was named Janet. She explained the twelve-step program and told us that to join the "sober" school a child had to complete sixty days sober. Ryan had neared sixty days by that time, so we set a time to meet with Janet again and bring him with us. She recommended that I attend a twelve-step parent meeting before our date with Ryan, to learn about twelve-step healing myself. This was a recovery for me also, and I needed to step to the next phase. I hoped that Lauren would be willing to step to her next phase, which would include recovery. Instead, she got nastier with me during this time. She broke curfew often, but because I was still attending Tough Love, I was still imposing consequences on her. When Lauren didn't come home at night, Bob helped me take the door off her bedroom. We also moved her furniture to the back yard patio to make it clear that her life was not her own—we operated as a family.

These consequences led to times when Lauren would just want to talk to Bob and me, seeming so open and communicative; however, I noticed new behaviors that were odd. She stayed up late at night, obsessively cleaning her room. In the morning she was like a dead weight when I would try to wake her up for school. I also noticed her weight dropping again and her moods fluctuating to extremes. Lauren was only euphoric or horribly nasty. Amazingly, during this time she remained consistent with church and continued to go to confirmation classes until she graduated. We confirmed her in the spring that year. She could be so inconsistent at home and school, yet follow through on church commitments, so I could only address incidents as they arose. One Saturday I walked by her room and saw something shiny under her bed, which ended up being an empty fifth of vodka. Upon further investigation I discovered more empty bottles in her room. When I was done, I had a large black garbage bag filled with empty liquor bottles she had been keeping right under my nose.

When Lauren returned home, I was there with the evidence waiting to greet her. She had just come from church, and when I confronted her, she stared at me blankly and said the bottles weren't hers. I grounded her for two weeks, but it didn't seem to accomplish anything. She isolated herself in her room and treated me like I had the plague. Another time I found a marijuana pipe sitting on her desk, and when she came home found me again, along with a police officer. He had a firm discussion with her, warning her that next time he would take her to jail, but once again this made her furious and then withdrawn. Lauren blamed me for ruining her life. Nothing seemed to work with her, and I was beyond my tolerance levels, running on overwhelm. I was stressed and frustrated and so very tired of it all.

One Sunday afternoon my hope shrank back further still. Shirley called and asked if she could come and talk to me about something. When she arrived, she told me that her daughter, Lindsey, had confessed that Lauren had been heavily using crystal meth. Lindsey was upset that Lauren was getting into drugs so heavily and told her mother because she was worried Lauren might end up dead. I was furious at Shirley for acting like she had the inside scoop on what was going on with Lauren. I couldn't believe that she would take Lindsey's story at face value. I was sure that this was something that Lindsey had just made up to take the focus off being in whatever trouble she was in with her mother at that time. I listened and thanked Shirley for her information, but inside I was seething. *How dare Lindsey make up something like this about Lauren*, I repeated in my head.

Denial is such a potent and all-consuming state of consciousness. It is a dangerous flipside of hopefulness. It protects us from what is too painful for us to acknowledge. The trick is not to stay there. That afternoon after Shirley left, I had to take a good hard look at how I was dealing with the news I had received about Lauren. My conscious mind did not want to comprehend what I knew in my heart was probably true. The beast of my grandfather's and father's and mine was now hers in a way I could no longer deny. My daughter was addicted to a drug I had been addicted to also, and I heard myself keep asking, "How could this be happening?" I got down on my knees in my bedroom and prayed. I was scared to death that if I did not do something, Lauren would end up dead just as Lindsey had feared.

Lauren didn't know at that time that I had also had a problem with crystal meth at her age. I wonder if I should have been more candid about my past. I became so close to the situation after Lauren's addiction began to include meth, I felt like I was being punished personally for having hid my secret from her. I asked myself how my daughter could end up having a major problem with the exact same drug, but at least part of the answer was because I had never told Lauren that she comes from an addicted family. I had to do something, or the legacy of addiction was never going to end. I picked up the phone and called the adolescent drug group, where Lauren had been with me for family counseling when Ryan was attending. I sat her down and talked with her about it, and I said that if she did not want to get sober, she would have to find another place to live. I was no longer going to tolerate drug use in my home.

Demanding that Lauren listen to me or get out of my house was one of the hardest things I had ever done. The last thing I wanted was for her to end up on the streets, but I also knew if I continued to allow her to carry on, Lauren might likely die. She agreed that day to go to the intake session, a relief that made me feel grateful for Shirley, not angry at her anymore. I sat in the waiting room while Lauren talked to the counselor, wishing that whatever happened in there, she would be willing to accept help. I knew I had to allow her to make her own decision, to help us both in the long run. The counselor came out and said that she was very sorry, but Lauren was not willing to get sober or attend the drug group, which left me with a feeling of despair. Right when I had thought I had been given a chance to turn things around, again it all felt like a waste of time.

I had to follow through on my promise to Lauren, that if she continued to use drugs I would ask her to leave the house, so we drove home in silence, and I asked Lauren where she would like me to drop her off. She asked if she could pack a few things at the house first and make a phone call. I agreed. Lauren got on the phone with her best friend, Paige, who had moved to Wisconsin. At nine in the evening I had to pick Ryan up from his meeting and had planned to drop Lauren off someplace when I returned. Just as I was leaving to get him, Lauren came running out after me. She asked if she could go with me to pick Ryan up. I was suspicious. I thought maybe she was just trying to stall so she didn't have to leave, which was most likely the case given her history of excuses. I took her anyway, and when we arrived at the meeting, about fifty teens were outside the coffee shop, just like the first time Bob and I had visited the twelve-step center. More and more kids poured out of the meeting that had just let out. They were running around talking, laughing, and having fun. Lauren's eyes opened wide. I could see disbelief on her face as she watched the crowd of kids, all having the time of their lives. She said, "Wow, I could be a leader in this group. Mom, let me out of the car." I unlocked the door, and the next thing I knew she was lost in a crowd of teens.

Lauren could be so incredibly consistent and focused when she was committed to something. That was a quality that I admired in her and hoped she would develop as she matured. I studied her face that night, as she stood talking in the crowd around her, knowing that my real daughter was inside her somewhere. If only her focus could shift from drugs to a group like the kids in the twelve-step program, then perhaps there was hope. I sat patiently in my car with that thought for about fifteen minutes, waiting for Ryan and Lauren. I noticed Ryan was talking to a boy whom we had known from the adolescent drug group. The boys walked over to the car, and Ryan's friend proceeded to tell me, proudly, that he had thirty days sober. He said he had never been able to stay sober in the other programs, which made him enthusiastic about doing great. Lauren got back in the car shortly after and looked at me and said, "Mom, I want to be in this program." I turned and gushed, "Okay!" I wanted the same hope for Lauren that I had seen in the eyes of Ryan's friend.

HEALING FROM THE BOTTOM UP

CHAPTER 5

My first twelve-step parent meeting was pretty frustrating. One of my new rules was supposed to have been that Lauren and Ryan attend meetings with me, and I ended up driving to the meeting by myself. I just didn't have it in me that night to drag them there. Lauren said she had a headache, and Ryan complained of both a headache and a stomachache. When I walked into the room, I felt so much like an outsider. Many of the people were laughing and talking happily. I didn't understand it. These were all parents of addicts. How were they able to look so happy? They must be insane, I thought, or they had a different kind of kids than mine. I had to stand and tell the group my name. After I did, I realized I wasn't the only new parent there, or the only other parent who was overwhelmed. I was welcomed with clapping and cheering. Each of us had a chance that night to talk and tell about our present situation. I told the group about what I had been going through with Lauren and Ryan. The lady leading the meeting looked at me, smiled, and said, "At least you are here!"

I was taken into a special meeting for newcomers after I met with the group, where I was given information about the twelve-step process. The concept of "enthusiastic sobriety" was explained to me, and the two-year program time line for teen sobriety was laid out to show me that sobriety could be taught as an attractive way of life. The philosophy of enthusiastic sobriety included having fun, sticking with sober people, and having honesty and integrity in relationships. It basically promoted getting children off drugs by teaching them to think straight and take their lives back. At the foundation of enthusiastic sobriety was the twelve-step recovery process, a set of guiding principles for recovery from various addictions.

The twelve-step process was originally developed by the fellowship of Alcoholics Anonymous (AA), for the recovery of alcoholism. Working the twelve steps involves admitting that one cannot control one's addiction, recognizing a greater power that can give strength, examining past errors with the help of a sponsor who is an experienced member of a twelve-step group, making amends for past errors, learning to live a new life with a new set of behaviors, and helping others that suffer from the same addictions. The teens in twelve-step with Ryan were going to be encouraged to stick with "winners" only, which meant other sober people. Peer groups, I was told, were so important to a teenager that recovery could only happen when kids stopped hanging around with their former drug-using friends.

This was the first time I was told that drug abuse and alcoholism were both diseases, and that each was progressive and deadly enough that these risks, not behavior issues, were the focus of the program. It was a total change from the way we had approached Lauren and Ryan's addictions. The concept at twelve-step was to get a teen off the substances first, so that many of the other behaviors would start to fall in place. In addition to this education for the kids, the twelve-step center did some individual counseling and held outpatient sessions. Next door to that was the coffee shop, where the teens could hang out or host functions and dances. The program also had an inpatient unit available, if that was necessary. The counselors who ran the inpatient program were different from any professionals I had met. All of them were young adults that were recovering themselves. Most had gotten sober in the twelve-step program. I suspected this was what had led to the impressive success rate of the program with teens.

It was recommended that parents come to meetings while their children were in the program, to reinforce the successes of counseling. I was committed to doing that. The teen group for Lauren and Ryan would include kids up to age eighteen. A young adult group also met, which included people through the age of twenty-four, but the program was typically two years long, after which time group members were encouraged to stay in touch and begin attending other twelve-step meetings. All of what I heard that first night made sense to me. The parent who led the group told her story, about her daughter's behavior, drug abuse, and constant running away. Attempting to manage this had made her a mother who was completely out of control. As I listened, all I could think was, *Wow, I can relate to that.* She was telling my story.

The night closed with an appointment I had to make to schedule Lauren and Ryan for their evaluations. They each spoke with the senior counselor at the twelve-step center individually. "Well," she said to me after they finished up, "they are willing to give this a try." She had explained to them that they would be expected to attend two meetings per week and all social functions. If I ran into problems, I was to contact her. She reminded me of the commitment I also needed to make. "It's really important that you commit to attending the parent meetings," she said. "It can make all the difference if you are working on getting healthy, too. This is a family disease, and it affects everyone in the household."

After blowing off that first meeting, Lauren and Ryan did make it to their own meetings during our first month, although they refused to go to coffee after their meetings, or to the social functions that they had promised they would attend. I spoke to the counselors about this. They didn't think it was unusual because Lauren and Ryan were so new to twelve-step. Ryan had only just graduated to twelve-step from recovery. Lauren had only caught the fire for the program after seeing all the kids Ryan had met in the group. Sometimes I took them home after their meeting and went to be with the parents I had met. I didn't really like leaving the kids home alone, because we were still having issues, but the counselors assured me that I could not watch them constantly. If issues were going to come up, it was best to let them happen, and then we could deal with them together.

I shared the negative reactions from Lauren and Ryan, about the coffee shop and social functions, with the parents in my meetings. "You can't expect miracles overnight," one man said to me. "Progress is that they are attending two meetings per week with some really cool people. They'll come around." After listening to my parent group, I brought my anger to them, so that the other parents could help me learn to respond, instead of reacting at Lauren and Ryan for not participating. Gradually, this system paid off. They started to go to coffee after the meetings, but I could sense they were still unsure. Addiction still had them and was still fighting to be the most important thing in their lives.

The first major crack in our new program was with Ryan. He disappeared for an entire twenty-four hours, after which I found him passed out in his bedroom reeking of marijuana and alcohol. Counselors at twelve-step recommended that he go through the outpatient program, which was a forty-five-day treatment, after we found him. I agreed that it would be the best choice, and a counselor from twelve-step came to the house to help me take Ryan in. She went into his bedroom and woke him up. Together they went outside on the patio and talked for about fifteen minutes. She performed a drug intervention right under my own roof, which had never happened before. The first week of outpatient went pretty well for him, but on the weekend he hooked up with a drug buddy. Once again, I found drugs at my house. The first thing I did the following week was call Ryan's outpatient counselor. He said, "Thank you! We will deal with this." I was proud of myself because I never mentioned to Ryan I had found his drugs. I worked as a teammate with the counselors, who had promised I could rely on them, and together we were confronting the obstacles we faced.

It was the obstacles with Ryan that led to the discoveries about Lauren. Despite her slow startup with the twelve-step group, she had actually been headed in the opposite direction still and hadn't reached her bottom yet. I came to a pivotal realization about reaching bottom with the program counselors, through Ryan's subsequent slides. I had returned to denial to cope after two weekends in particular with him that had gone very badly. The worst of it was when a policeman found Ryan on a golf course and explained he believed Ryan was under the influence of some type of illegal drug. It was two in the morning, and we all stood on my doorstep looking at Ryan. His eyes were black and dilated. He was supposed to have been out at a "sober" party. I told the whole story to Ryan's counselor, trying to convince him that the policeman may have been wrong about the drugs. The counselor looked at me and said, "If it walks like a duck and talks like a duck, it's a duck. Your son is a drug addict, and all of the evidence points to the fact that he is still actively using."

The counselor was getting at the fact that for an addict, change does not come until life circumstances force the addiction to hit a bottom. That bottom clearly had not been reached with Ryan, because it was possible for him to return to a safe home after continuing to get busted. I just sighed and closed my eyes after hearing the news. I knew Ryan's counselor was right. "You're going to make me go there, aren't you?" I asked him. He wanted my help to make Ryan's drug use as uncomfortable as possible. I had been there before, with Lauren, and I knew that this was a tremendously hard place for a mother. I got the recommendation to give Ryan a jar of peanut butter, a loaf of bread, some change to make a phone call, and his counselor's phone number. I was supposed to let the counselor do the rest. He was going tell to Ryan that the only place he was welcome from now on was at the inpatient unit at the hospital run by the twelve-step group.

Ryan didn't agree to enter inpatient. I had the peanut butter, bread, and the pocket change all ready when he got home. "Well," he said, "you know I don't like this running away stuff, so I'll be living in the back yard." "Uh-huh," I said and walked back into the house. I was serious and ready. By that time I had my parent group, a supportive boyfriend, and lots of support from the counselors we were working with. I ran to my room and called one of the parents on my meeting phone list to talk. She told me that she was proud of me and that she would see me at the meeting that night. Thank goodness there was a meeting that day. I sure needed it. When I told the others in my small group that Ryan was living in the back yard, everyone started laughing, and I found myself joining in. Laughing in the middle of a major crisis turned out to feel really good. That was the week I heard the news about Lauren. After he had spent an hour on the phone with his sponsor, Ryan had agreed to go into the hospital. "He just cried so much that I didn't know what to do with him the first couple of days. Then I realized that he felt bad about himself, so I encouraged him to give himself a chance," said the counselor who worked with him. Soon after, Ryan called me himself. "Mom," he started, "I decided that I want to be sober. I am doing really well, but I have a problem. I can't come home because my sister is still using drugs."

I felt my heart sink when I heard this news, but I knew it was true. I felt so happy for Ryan, but that happiness led directly to a worry about Lauren, because she hadn't hit the bottom that Ryan had hit. No one is ever healed or cured from the illness of addiction, but it does go into remission, and there is ongoing healing through recovery in remission for an addict who has reached the lowest low and knows the terrible feeling of that place. To get Ryan home, I had to deal with Lauren. I decided to meet with the counselors to discuss what to do. I knew in my heart it was going to take more than a twelve-step program for her to choose sobriety. She had a drug dealer boyfriend who was actively using. She spent most of her time with friends that used drugs. She was not going to give this world up easily. Lauren's bottom would need to be extreme.

Lauren had continued to go to the twelve-step group after Ryan entered the hospital. She told everyone that she had decided to be sober. She claimed to have several weeks of sobriety; however, she was still hanging around with her old drug friends. Something inside of me felt uneasy about it all. Just her word that she was sober didn't mean anything anymore. Counselors at the twelve-step center had been discussing Lauren's situation, because it had become obvious by then that she was living a lie. They told me that there were some new possibilities in the program and that they would like me to come in and talk about these. I told them Bob, his kids, and I had plans to go away that weekend, but I assured the counselors I knew it was important to talk and I would make the time. I didn't think I would be more than an hour. Four hours after Lauren and I showed up to talk to the counselors, we returned home, where Bob was at the house waiting with his daughters, all packed up to go.

Bob understood, because so much had already happened with the counselors and Lauren. She had been asked to go next door when we arrived at the meeting, into the coffee shop where the kids hung out, which meant I was in for major news. Our counselor told me that a ten-bed residential inpatient house was due to open and asked if I would consider putting Lauren in as one of the first patients. I quickly thought about practicalities, like how much the program would cost, because I didn't know if it would be covered by insurance. The counselor told me financial options were available and that the executive director of the residential house would discuss these with me if I decided to give Lauren a try there. After talking to that director, I realized I could do it and that I really needed to at least consider it as a step to offer Lauren toward recovery, rather than the lows she had been sinking to. It took four hours at the meeting because I went to the residential house that day, to check it out. "The person who will be running the administration is out there now," I was told. If I wanted to, I could sign Lauren up.

I closed my eyes, listening for a reaction from my body, and everything in me told me that placing Lauren in the residential house was the right thing to do. The counselors had been busy while I was gone. I had said yes to their offer to do a drug intervention with Lauren. While I was on my way thirty miles across town to visit the residential facility, her counselors were confronting her. I was emotional and tearful as I drove but through these emotions continued to experience a sensation of calmness despite how fast everything was moving. When I walked into the residential facility, I felt the power in the moment. It was as if I was standing in the exact right place, at the exact right moment that I needed to have been standing there. I was able to tell the administrator of the residential program about my struggles in the past, and she shared her journey of recovery with me. Both of us talked about Lauren. "She sounds like such a wonderful, strong girl with so many possibilities. We would love to have her here," she said. Hearing this, I felt a flood of emotion come over me, and I started to cry.

The phone rang while I was at the residential house, and it was the twelve-step center calling to report back about the intervention with Lauren. I was afraid to hear the news. Lauren had agreed to come into treatment under two conditions. She wanted to go on the camping trip with Bob and his kids and me, and she wanted to finish her last two days of school before she was admitted. I asked the administrator of the residential house what I should do. "Take her camping and love her," she told me. She told me to praise Lauren for making a tough decision and trust her to follow through. "Don't let her see your fear," she said. "Hit your knees and pray, and trust God to do the rest. Go have fun this weekend. You are doing great." Lauren didn't think so. When I picked her up after my visit to the residential house, I found her on the curb at the twelve-step center, sitting with an angry face. She got in the car, closed the door hard, and gave me a hateful look.

"Don't be mad at me," I said bluntly. "It wasn't my idea." When I took myself out of the equation, her mouth dropped, and her face changed to a very pensive expression. This was a major shift in her reactions toward me that was a direct result of the concepts I had learned in my parents group. The meetings had taught me that addicts blame those they are closest to for everything going wrong in their lives, which in turn gives them more excuses to get high. I was not responsible for the fact that Lauren had ended up having a drug intervention that day. It was a direct result of her behavior. Arguing with her that the intervention was all her fault would have just made her throw it back in my face, so I didn't even begin that conversation. By pointing out the fact that her behavior had prompted the counselors to recommend the intervention, I diffused the situation. Lauren was forced to face the reality that she was on the hook for her behavior, not me.

Lauren did end up joining Bob, his kids, and me for the camping trip. Her hateful face even turned softer eventually, after building a campfire, pitching a tent, hiking, and horseback riding. She also went to school to finish up the last days of classes she had wanted to attend. But on the final day of class she went to see her boyfriend, Robert, after school, and by three in the morning, when she wasn't home, I knew there was trouble, so I continually called Robert's house. No one answered. Finally, someone picked up the phone. The person held me on the line while checking to see if Lauren was still there. A groggy Lauren came to the phone, slurring her words. "I'm on my way to pick you up." I said into the receiver. "Whatever," she said in a nasty voice.

On the way over to pick her up, I got myself together. If we got in a big argument over her choice, she could use it as an excuse to not go to treatment like she had promised to do if she was able to go camping and get her final two days of school in. I decided that I would use the new tools I learned in my parents group to fetch Lauren without saying a word. I picked her up, and we drove home in silence, just like I planned. When we got home, I told her I loved her and I went to bed, leaving her to sort out her own mess. I took the next day off work, and I heard signs of life in Lauren's bedroom around nine in the morning. She looked pretty hungover when she walked out. She took a shower, did her hair and makeup, and started to pack her things for the residential facility. Without my asking, she had kept her word to go into treatment.

At exactly one in the afternoon, Lauren's counselor pulled into the driveway to pick her up and take her to the residential facility. I hugged Lauren and told her I loved her and that I would see her at the meetings and functions at twelve-step. The car drove away from me, and I can remember what I felt like when I realized she was gone. I was so relieved as the car disappeared, even though I was crying. I went inside and collapsed on the couch. The stress I had been experiencing started to dissipate. I was thankful that both of my children had ended up safe and in good hands. The first few days after, things around my house were so quiet that it was bizarre for me. I got myself a sponsor, who was a parent in the group I had been attending. I told her I felt confused and fearful and couldn't understand why. She told me that I was experiencing normal feelings and recommended I be good to myself, take advantage of this time, and have some fun. The counselors agreed when I talked to them. They encouraged me to let them worry about my children and to let myself finally have a life.

I began to think in capital letters: WOW. I had actually received permission to be happy and let go of worrying and the fear of being angry. I decided it might not be such a bad idea to try that out, and I gave myself permission to let go. I made plans with Bob and other friends during this time. I went shopping, to the movies, and for hikes, and everything was wonderful. Updates came about Lauren's progress. "She is opening up a little, but she has a long way to go," I heard. It wasn't quite the miracle turnaround I had hoped for, but it was only the first week. Two days later I got the news that we did have a long way to go, indeed. Her counselor confessed Lauren had run away. During group she was confronted on her sobriety date, because other kids in the group felt she was being dishonest. Lauren got angry and ran out the door and across the street to the convenience store, where she was making phone calls when the executive director of the residential house confronted her. I couldn't imagine this story was going to be the start of another failure for us. No. It would have been too painful. "She decided to come back, but she is really upset," her counselor said. "Things are very shaky with her right now. We will keep you updated." *So much for my fun and happy times,* I thought to myself.

Fear washed over me when this occurred with Lauren. I had been getting way too comfortable. I began to get anxious again about what was going to happen next, yet there was nothing I could do about it. The day after Lauren ran away the first time, I received a second call from the residential facility. "I am sorry to tell you that Lauren ran away again today, and we just let her go this time. We'll be contacting you to let you know about your refund amount." I hurried to say, "Wait! You mean you're not going to try to talk her into coming back?" The voice at the other end of the line said no. Where the bottom will be really is the addict's own choice. I was told that for Lauren to return again, it would have to be her decision. This devastated me. I feared she would never make the choice to return, and if I couldn't force her to go back, I didn't know what options were left for us. My heart raced, and I felt like I couldn't breathe. I closed the door to my office, and I got down on my knees to find my center, begging, "Please . . . Lauren needs the courage to go back, and if not, help me to accept this choice and give me strength."

I made a call to my sponsor at that point, to get the support I needed over the phone. I spent the afternoon working, praying, and thinking. I could no longer support Lauren in her decisions if she stayed away from treatment, and I readied myself to tell her that she was no longer welcome in my home. I was really worried and very sad. All I did that day was get by. Just before I left work for the day, my phone rang. It was Lauren. "Hi, Mom, I'm at home," she said. "I left the program today, but don't worry, I decided to go back." My heart felt a surge of hope. I considered whether Lauren's choice to leave the residential house, as hard as it had been for me, actually might have been a good thing. Instead of being forced into treatment, Lauren had made the decision to choose recovery for herself.

I learned that she had called the counseling office, and they had asked her to phone me and tell me to bring Lauren to the coffee shop that night. "Okay," I told her when I heard the plan. "I will be home in a while."

No sooner had I hung up than the phone rang again. Her counselor had called me, to confirm that Lauren wanted to come back and that her group planned to meet Lauren at the coffee shop. However, the counselor added, "We are not just going to take her back. She is going to have to make some commitments to the group about sobriety and honesty. If she is not willing to do that, then she will not be welcome. This is not going to be an easy night for her." I thanked her for this information and finalized the plan to bring Lauren to the twelve-step center at the agreed-upon time. Bob and I went together to drop her off. We waited at the coffee shop while the group took Lauren into the therapy room to talk. When she came out, she looked pale and shook-up. "I'm going back with them," she said. I told her I loved her, and Bob and I left. A week later I received an update call, confirming that Lauren was doing incredibly well. I listened for a sign of trouble in her counselor's voice, but there wasn't that sound. "She has done a complete turn-around. She is telling her story and getting honest."

I couldn't believe what I had heard. I started to cry at the news of each additional detail. "Not only has she decided to be sober, she has also decided to give up all of her drug friends and is writing a letter to her boyfriend to break up with him. This was her idea and decision. We didn't even bring it up. We are very excited for her." So many emotions took me over as I listened. I felt gratitude, relief, joy, and elation. I could barely speak. I thanked the counselor and got off the phone. I saw Lauren that night at the coffee shop, after our meetings, and I was amazed. I noticed she was smiling and hugging people. You couldn't miss her across the room. She looked happy, and her face was glowing. When she saw me she yelled, "Mom!" I knew I had my daughter back. It was time for us to start up from the bottom. When she reached me, Lauren hugged me, told me that she loved me, and said she wanted to introduce me to some of her new friends. We held each other that night and cried together. I told her I loved her. That night, I was very proud to be her mom.

LIFE WITH EARLY SOBRIETY

CHAPTER 6

AFTER LAUREN REENTERED the residential house, our lives did not immediately turn around. Addiction causes a ripple effect for everyone who is involved. Problems that Lauren created early on began to unfold on us before they vanished on our shore of recovery. The coast was clear at least for Ryan to come home. I was happy and relieved to be able to have him back. He stayed busy at the twelve-step center with meetings, hanging out at the coffee shop, and running around town having fun with kids from the teen group. I actually didn't see him very often, and for the first time that felt okay.

The twelve-step program provided a lot of structure for the kids. Sunday was the only day during the week when there wasn't something major going on with the group. The counselors encouraged me to use Sunday as our family day, and I did so by always making an effort to do something fun with Lauren and Ryan. Sometimes their new friends would come along. It seemed there was always someone coming to the house for something, to pick up one of the kids or drop one off. I even had a stocked shelf in the refrigerator and a cupboard in the kitchen with food and snacks because I would often come home from work and find a group of young people at our home watching television, playing cards, or just sitting around talking. They were all so enthusiastic. It was contagious, and I loved being around them. The teens called me Mom. These kids were respectful and considerate and treated all the parents in our group the same way they treated me. There was rarely an occasion when the kids from twelve-step weren't willing to help out or clean up after themselves.

Bob and I attended parent meetings together during this time, continuing to show up for coffee afterward. I loved being in the atmosphere of the twelve-step coffee shop, because of the positive way kids interacted with adults. That amazing experience I had encountered on the first night I was exposed to this group became my daily reality after Lauren went back to inpatient and Ryan was back with us. This was such a drastic contrast to the way our lives had been previous to this program. Life seemed almost surreal. I saw Lauren on the nights we went to the coffee shop. Every time I saw her, it seemed that she had become happier and more content with the decision she had made to be sober. I still sometimes felt panicky, fearing that something bad was going to happen. It felt like I was a survivor of trauma. Everything was suddenly better by this point, but I still had subconscious feelings of panic that sobriety for my kids was all going to end up being just a dream. I didn't want to wake back up to the nightmare of our legacy of addiction.

My sponsor encouraged me to allow myself to experience the joy of this time in my life, and to connect with my sense of relief, but she also cautioned me that life was not going to become suddenly perfect. Early sobriety carries challenges, in large part due to unresolved issues about trust and self-confidence and the strings that an addict must cut from former relationships. I needed to start learning to trust Lauren and remember that things had happened with her exactly as they were supposed to. I didn't think she would go back to her old life at that point, but who knew? I also suspected that her old friends would come looking for her—our ripple effect. It was an easy decision to change our phone to an unlisted number, even though Lauren had broken her ties to these people. I put my feet on the ground with all this knowledge, just as my counselor suggested, and chose to live one day at a time.

We had to address Ryan's habit of stealing. I noticed something shiny under his bed one day when I walked by his room. I took a closer look, and I found a stash of very expensive power tools. I called my sponsor to tell her and to ask for guidance. She gave me some advice, telling me to go to Ryan directly and set a time line for the removal of the stolen things from my house. I followed through. When I saw Ryan at the coffee shop on the day I found the tools, I pulled him aside for a chat. I informed him I found property in his bedroom that did not belong to us. I told Ryan I wanted it removed from our home within twenty-four hours. He looked at me wide-eyed, with the color draining from his face, and said okay. Bob and I spotted Ryan sitting outside with his sponsor when we left. They were having a private talk, and Ryan looked pretty shook-up. The following evening I arrived home to find Ryan and his sponsor pulling out of our driveway, with the car loaded up with the tools. I heard later through the grapevine that they had returned the equipment to a construction site, where it had originally been taken from.

It felt good to see we were finding new solutions as a family to former, destructive patterns. I had done the right thing by talking to Ryan to let him know I found the stolen property, and setting a time line for it to be removed had caused him to react. He had done the right thing by working through the issue with the help of his sponsor and returning the equipment. Neither of us resorted to panicking or yelling during the incident. It was one of the first times that I realized I could give a problem to my child to solve instead of taking that problem on as my own, which only forced a solution that never allowed a chance for Lauren or Ryan to play a successful role they could be proud about.

Encouraging things also happened in my dynamics with Lauren. About a month into her inpatient stay, I received a phone call from her counselor to tell me that a special time had been made for me to sit in on a counseling session with Lauren, at which she could make amends for her past behavior. This was a special session every kid in the program was able to have, when the time was right. Because Lauren had made huge strides after her return to the residential house, she had been chosen to be the first person to have this type of meeting. I went alone, because I felt Lauren might be uncomfortable having Bob there. At that time he was sort of playing the role of dad to the kids, but to them he was still just my boyfriend. I didn't have a chance to ask Rick if he would have liked to go. In the time after Ryan had stopped living with his dad in Cottonwood, I hadn't heard much from Rick. He had been sent to prison for driving under the influence again.

When I arrived at the residential house for Lauren's session, I was taken into a room first, to meet privately with the founder of the program. He told me that he was excited about Lauren's progress. He explained the purpose of the meeting and told me to be open and to listen to what she had to say. He also asked after me. The founder was blunt and asked if I had a problem with alcohol or drugs. I told him no. I let him know that I was at the point with my drinking where I had only an occasional couple of glasses of wine. He seemed satisfied with this answer. Something in my head went off after I finished what I had to say, however. I felt an alert that I should reconsider my answer and say more, so I did. I told the founder about my past history, and his eyes got wide. I continued, "Well, there was that time that I almost died when I overdosed on crystal meth at the age of eighteen." He slapped his open palm loudly on the table and said, "You need to be sober!" I was dumbfounded. I didn't think I was totally sober but I still hadn't been aware that I might be an addict, too. It stunned me to face the possibility and weight of this revelation.

I knew I had been a child of an addict, and that I had married one, but I never once considered that I might be one after all the changes I had made. I drank moderately, but I didn't binge like I had in the past. I didn't abuse alcohol and hadn't touched an illegal drug in years. This confusion was all over my face. The founder noticed it and said, "Let me give you an example. You are at a party and you have had your two or three glasses of wine. You go upstairs to use the bathroom and walk by a bedroom where they are cutting out lines of crystal meth. What are you going to do?" I didn't think that story was very likely to happen in my life any longer, but I really could not tell him I was sure that if it did I wouldn't be drawn back to my former habit. Relapse happens to addicts. I promised to quit on my own one time, and it was only one night out drinking with friends that had taken me back into doing drugs. I had to admit I had had major problems with drugs and alcohol in the past. I didn't have anything to lose by giving them up altogether.

It was the next step in my family's journey for all of us to be completely sober and clean. I said okay to the founder, and that day now marks my sobriety date. It was a surprise when it happened, that like Lauren did that night, I also made some intense confessions. I went to my session with her and was led into a room with the other kids in her inpatient group. Ten kids were there, and Lauren addressed us all. She told me how sorry she was for all that she had put me through. She said she had been hard at work on herself by staying sober and making sure her actions were clean. She communicated that she was willing to "stick with winners" now and was in the process of changing the people she surrounded herself with. Lauren told me that night that she wanted our relationship to be better. She was working to earn back my trust. So much more had happened to us both than I was expecting when I arrived at the session.

I was filled with gratitude and pride for Lauren's willingness to change her life. I tearfully accepted her amends and hugged her tightly when the session was done. I couldn't have wished for a better outcome. Two weeks later was her graduation day from the residential home and her return to our house, which made me nervous and excited, all at the same time. I bought her a bouquet of flowers, which I put on her bed. It was great to have her in the house again because it gave me a sense of gratitude to see my family under one roof, finally back together. Lauren entered into six weeks of an intensive outpatient program following her graduation. It took her away from the house for six hours per day. She was sometimes gone even more than that because new friends would come and whisk her away. Some of these new friendships were very deep, and I could see that Lauren was reaching out beyond herself in a positive way.

At the residential house, she had befriended a girl named Tara. Lauren approached me about the possibility of Tara living with us, so that both girls could attend the outpatient program together after graduation. Tara's family was willing to provide money for room and board and for Tara's extra needs. I was fine with that arrangement, and Tara moved in. Outpatient was supposed to be a safe place for her and Lauren, and I hardly worried that either of them would run into any problems there if they completed the program together. The two of them together didn't, but Lauren did on her own because of her former boyfriend, Robert. He had showed up at the twelve-step center looking for her. When he did, staff there told Robert to leave and not come back. For fear of upsetting Lauren at this new phase of her sobriety, nobody told Lauren and instead told me, just to make me aware of the problem.

Staff suggested that I sit down with Lauren and tell her what was happening when the two of us could talk at home. She was very upset when I shared the news. Lauren demanded to know why no one had informed her that Robert had showed up at twelve-step. She was distressed because if her safety was at issue, she should have been told about that fact at group. I also informed her that I had gone to the police station that day to file a restraining order against Robert. I did this to protect myself and Lauren. Robert might have brought drugs and chaos back into our lives again. It felt important to do something concrete that could stop that possibility.

Several nights later, Lauren and Tara had rented the movie *Scream*, a slasher flick. I recommended that they not watch it, with everything that had gone on with Robert, but they decided to watch the movie anyway, late that night with all of the lights off. I was in my bedroom drifting off to sleep when I heard Robert's banging. Lauren was in a panic. "Oh my god, oh my god, Robert is banging on the front window." She was screaming while I tried to remain calm and settle the girls down. I called the police, and we sat silently in the dark, hiding until they arrived. *How dare Robert come around disrupting our lives*, I remember fuming, *trying to drag Lauren back into his drug-infested world*. I felt like a mama bear protecting her cubs. Anger filled me all the way up.

When the police arrived, there was no sign of Robert. He had disappeared, and the police noted that there was not much they could do anyway, besides warn him, if Robert was ever found. Several nights later he might have come by again. Tara was home by herself and had taken a shower. She went into Lauren's room to change, and apparently the blinds were slightly open. She was naked when she looked at the window to see a man standing outside staring back at her. She screamed, grabbed a towel to wrap around her body, and ran through the house to get away. Tara made her way to the kitchen, where she grabbed a large knife out of a kitchen drawer and held it tightly as she lay on the couch in a fetal position. Ryan found her that way when he came home several hours later. When I arrived home, Tara told me the story and described a man who fit the description of Robert.

We called the police after this happened. Again, we reported Robert. Apparently the police had run across him and chatted with him about our complaints, but he denied everything and claimed he had an alibi. Later in the week we received papers in the mail that informed us that Robert was fighting our restraining order. Because of his choice, we had to appear in court if we wanted the order to stand. Lauren was petrified at this prospect. On the day of the hearing she did not want to see Robert and had definitely said she did not want to have to testify against him. Her counselor had recommended that she have one of the other counselors accompany her to court for support, and so we also took that counselor with us. Bob came, too. We led ourselves courageously into the courtroom to protect our sober world.

Together, we had a league of sober people standing strong against Robert. Even with all this support, Lauren remained distraught. She told us that she was not going to be able to go through with it. An upset Bob reminded her that he did not think that was an option. "Lauren, if you don't do this, you will always be looking over your shoulder," he said. "Not only will this put you at risk, but your mother and your brother could be in danger as well." The situation was bigger than her was what he was trying to say. It involved all of us, which Lauren was able to see after she considered our situation. Because she had become sober, she had reconnected to her sense of family and was determined to help us all stay on track. Lauren agreed to testify against Robert, and we went to the courtroom together.

The judge asked Robert to explain why he thought that the restraining order should be overturned. He stated it should be overturned because he had never tried to contact Lauren after receiving her letter, the one she wrote to indicate to him that she wanted to break up. Robert said he wanted Lauren to be happy and wanted what was best for her. The judge then listened to Lauren's account of the incidents that had occurred. The two stories were obviously very different. The judge did not try to determine which story was true. Instead, he told Robert that if he was truly only interested in Lauren's best interests and had no intention of contacting her any longer, then to let the restraining order against him stand should not be any problem. We were all very relieved at the final outcome. "Your request is denied," the judge told Robert. Robert was visibly unhappy and left the courtroom with his cousin. That was the last we would ever hear from him.

Life got into a smooth rhythm with Lauren after that. She remained heavily involved with twelve-step. Work, meetings, and continuing to develop my relationship with Bob were what consumed my time. There was also a special group I joined for adults with addiction issues because of the decision I had made about my past addictions. The first night at my new meeting, I was asked to share about myself. I revisited some of my history. After hearing myself talk, I realized there was no question I had found a place that was exactly where I needed to be. I felt shaky and scared for the first few months of my sobriety. Those couple of glasses of wine I was occasionally drinking before this time had just seemed enough to take the edge off. The knowledge I could no longer medicate myself in that way was frightening, but the others in the meeting told me to just keep coming back. As I continued to attend, I started to feel hopeful. I learned about the same twelve steps that were healing Ryan and Lauren and began using those steps for myself.

Each ripple that would meet us continued to die out. Eventually the ripples would hit the shore of recovery and break. The troubles we did have were about personal relationships now, instead of problems with drugs, guns, the police, or calls from school administrators. The relationship that caused me the most concern was between Lauren and a boy from twelve-step she had began dating, John. I wondered whether it was too early in her sobriety to be in a relationship. Self-confidence is hard for an addict to regain, and a bad relationship can function as a crutch in early sobriety, because confidence has yet to return. Lauren was eighteen by this time, though, and when she had eight months sober she celebrated her birthday, moved into an apartment with three other girls from the group, left the teen program, and moved on to join the young adults in recovery. She got a job and seemed to be doing well. My only worry was that she seemed to be getting more serious with John, and I noticed that it began to affect her recovery. Lauren started to miss meetings and functions.

She became very defensive when anyone questioned her absences. It was the same aggressive anger Lauren had shown me when she was defending her addictive behaviors. I received a call one day from one of the program counselors that had also begun to worry about the relationship between Lauren and John. Counselors felt the relationship had become unhealthy. I tried to talk to Lauren before counselors warned her, but she did not want to hear it. A week later, I received a call that she and John had not listened to the warnings from the counselors either, and the two of them had been asked to leave the program. *You've got to be kidding me*, I thought. Lauren had come up from the bottom, away from our family addiction to drugs and booze, only to stay caught up in the beast of a bad relationship. After all we had been through, we had found a place of stability through twelve-step, and now the stability was going to be removed.

I didn't trust that Lauren could function as well as she had if she was forced to function without the program, so I chose to make myself ready for what might come next, feeling very worried and sick. Her roommates informed Lauren that she was going to have to find a new place to live because she was no longer in the program. Lauren moved into the apartment of a former group member, who was also no longer with twelve-step. I didn't think things could get any worse when I received the call that Lauren was pregnant. "Mom, I have something to tell you," she started. She paused, and I held my breath. "You're going to be a grandma." I don't recall exactly what I said to her after I heard the news, but I felt like a train had hit me. I tried to stay calm until I could phone my sponsor for support. I thanked Lauren for telling me and asked her if she was okay. She said she was, and I somehow got off the phone.

I called my sponsor immediately after that, and my sponsor reminded me that I wasn't the one having the baby, Lauren was. I was continuing to work on my ability to let my kids handle their own lives. With the new baby Lauren was going to need me, but my sponsor was recommending that I not jump into the situation and try to fix it or control it. I had to let Lauren try. She was the one who would be faced with some tough decisions, and she would need my love and support, not my solutions. The best thing I could do, my sponsor said, was to just be a mom. I could love Lauren and pray for guidance in the situation. So that is what I did.

Several nights later I received a call from Lauren that she was on her way to the emergency room. She had experienced a sharp pain in her abdomen and was bleeding. Bob and I went to the hospital and stood by her side. She had not miscarried, but her doctor felt there was a good possibility she would. Lauren was ordered to rest for a few days, but I received a late-night call not long after that. Lauren was in pain again and bleeding, and John had refused to take her to the hospital. Bob got on the phone with John at that point and told him to take Lauren to the hospital immediately and to start taking some responsibility for what was going on. John didn't seem very interested in hearing what Bob had to say. It all fell on deaf ears. John hung up on Bob, and we didn't know where Lauren was or how to find her. We called the hospital a couple of hours later, but she was not there. We panicked at that news, hopped in the car, and started to make calls to find Lauren as we drove around looking for her.

A friend gave us an address where Lauren and John might have been staying. The drive there felt like an eternity. We had not been driving all night, but we had been up all night just trying to locate them. I was very upset and holding back tears most of the way. This was my daughter and my grandchild on the line. How dare John treat them the way he had? I went inside when Bob and I arrived at the address, only to find Lauren cramped over and in pain. She asked me to go into the bathroom with her. She was terrified and needed to show me the clot of blood that she had passed. It looked like a small fetus. We wadded it up in tissue and took it to the hospital with us, where Lauren was admitted into the emergency room and it was confirmed that she had miscarried. My heart broke for my daughter. She lay in the emergency room, having lost her baby, and her boyfriend was nowhere to be found.

Word spread among her friends that Lauren was in the hospital, and kids started showing up to visit her. John finally came but stood talking to a group of friends. I found out later that he never even went in to see Lauren. The saga of Lauren and John came to a bitter end at that point. After she was released from the hospital, Lauren had nowhere to go but back to the apartment she had been sharing with the friend who was also formerly part of twelve-step. When Bob and I went to visit her at this house, we were dismayed. The place was filthy, and garbage was strewn about. We had to kick our way through the debris just to walk in. Calling it a rat's nest would be an understatement. I was disgusted and discouraged. Lauren was sitting in a corner, up against a wall, because there was almost no furniture. She looked drawn and depressed. It was so hard for me to leave her there. I had to resist asking if I could take her home to make it all better, but I knew that I needed to allow her to work through the situation for herself.

Lauren had not been working while she lived at the apartment with her friend. Whenever I stopped by, she was sitting pretty much in the same place on the floor where she always sat. There were times she would call me in desperation, when she was hungry and had no food. I felt like someone was ripping my heart out of my chest. I didn't understand why Lauren would choose to live this way, after she had learned how to make so many other, good choices to change her otherwise destructive habits. I hadn't known how to make choices like that at Lauren's age. When I lived with Rick, he brought the homeless man to stay with us, or let our neighbor Jay shoot up in our living room, and I lived that way because I didn't know our life could be any different. I had lived surrounded by addiction and insane behavior all my life. Perhaps if I would have told Lauren more about my history, it may have shown her that she had learned things that were remarkable given our family story.

Sometimes when I came to visit her, I would just tell Lauren I loved her, and other times I would drop off a bag of fast food as an act of kindness. I thought about the types of resolutions that could potentially come to change her situation. The way she had chosen to live wouldn't last forever, but at the time it sure felt like it would. I remembered hearing from my sponsor and other parents in the program that when your kid is not okay, you're not okay. That was certainly true for me. I continued to go to my meetings. I worked on my program to stay positive. I chose to accept the love and support of Bob, and to trust that early addiction holds many challenges. I believed that the faith in personal change Lauren and I embraced in the twelve-step program would see her through. That kept me going more than anything during this dark time.

A couple of months after Lauren's miscarriage, I heard news that a reunion was going to be held to celebrate the first year of the residential house. Teens that had been through that program were invited to attend with their parents. Lauren got word about the reunion, too, and was told she was welcome to come, but she wasn't sure. My hope was high. On the morning of the reunion, I picked her up, and together with Bob we all made the drive to the inpatient program where Lauren had lived. She went directly in the house. Bob and I walked to the back yard to join the festivities. We did not see Lauren for quite some time, but when she finally came out where we were she had swollen, puffy eyes and a renewed look of hope on her face.

To know that early sobriety will lead to recovery, hope is an essential component. "I'm going to the dance at the coffee shop," Lauren told me that night at the reunion. She had learned that the beast of addiction is never as strong as any of us are after we decide we are capable of picking ourselves up at any time to try again. This choice would never have occurred to my father or to his dad. Both were too far removed from the challenges of facing real pain. When she was given the chance to try again, Lauren was relieved to say, "I'm also going to go back to the group." I wanted to jump up and down and scream with delight when I saw this determination after a run of discouragement for her that had been excruciating. I just nodded, like I had always known she could do it. I guess I had. I guess I knew that we had both broken a family legacy handed to us as if we weren't going to have a choice about it. Feelings of relief and gratitude flooded my whole being that night. Lauren and I had made a choice for hope. I smiled and told her, "Lauren, that's great."

PART II.

WATCHING MYSELF FALL

A Daughter's Story of Beating
the Legacy of Addiction

MY BEAST,
MY ADDICTION

CHAPTER 7

TRUST ME, it was no easy realization to figure out that I was an alcoholic and an addict, and that I had to choose hope and change if I planned to live. Over the course of my using, all my dreams had disappeared one by one. I was left with nothing to believe in but our family legacy of addiction. It was what I had seen around me growing up. Most people can remember and could tell you when and where they had their first beer or alcoholic beverage, but I honestly don't remember the first time that I tried alcohol because it's all a blur still. I can't recall my starting point. All I can remember is that once I started, I didn't stop for years.

I think of my addiction as a beast. My mother has told me that the beast began as a nightmare lived by her grandfather and father. It then came to her and passed on to my brother, Ryan, and me. Just maybe, if we are prone to addictive behaviors, we were born with this beast inside of us, and it lies dormant until we awaken it. Maybe, once the beast is awakened, it just wants to continue to thrive and grow. Mine did. When I experienced my first highs, I fell in love. I wanted to feel that way forever. From that moment on in my life, the beast wanted more and more. The more I fed my addiction, the bigger my beast grew. The more it would take to feed my beast, the less I could manage doing anything else, until feeding it became an endless cycle.

I never planned on becoming an alcoholic and a drug addict, though. I was so against the idea, and as a little girl I even swore to myself that I would never become like my father, Rick, an alcoholic. He put his booze before anyone or anything in his life. My needs as his child were always put on the back burner, and I never got the attention or love from him that I desperately needed. From as far back as I can remember, he loved two things: his alcohol and his women. My childhood perception of him was that he was a bottomless pit when it came to alcohol. He drank until he blacked out. Then he would wake up the next day and do it all over again. I knew I didn't want a life like that.

My father's famous line still rings in my head: "You kids want to go get a Pepsi?" That was the cue for Ryan and I to get ready for a long night at my dad's local dive. It didn't matter if we got there at noon or six in the evening; Ryan and I were stuck there for the rest of the night. We became pros at keeping entertained to pass the time watching our dad getting wasted. We learned how to play cards. We would get the bartender to give us the keys to the arcade games, so we didn't have to keep putting quarters in them, because heaven forbid we would use up all of dad's drinking money. There was no point in our trying to run through his resources. No matter how long we had been there already, we weren't leaving until he was good and ready.

That I ended up just as committed to my addiction as he was isn't surprising, considering that addiction is an illness that runs in families. Because the lifestyle is so familiar, it finds even the little girls like me who promise to never grow up and be as bad as their dad. My brother and I tried everything in the book to get him to change. We faked sick or told him we were ready for bed, but he still didn't budge from his bar stool. If we got too tired, we would just have to use the bar booths as our bed. When we were hungry, bar food became our dinner. After a while of his dragging us from bar to bar, I guess we just ended up in his way, because then he began to leave us home alone. He soon figured out that if he told us he was running to the store for a pack of cigarettes, we'd assume he was coming back, and we wouldn't try to tag along. Eventually he would call, hours later, letting us know that he had stopped off to get a drink, always assuring us that he was now on his way home, though he never really was.

When I was with my father I was lonely; I felt unwanted and abandoned. There were many nights when I didn't think I was going to live to see the next day. I dreaded the car rides home after he had spent the day at the bar. I can remember crying and begging my father not to drive. I would tell him that I was scared and that I didn't want to die. It was always my first priority to make sure that Ryan and I had our seat belts on. Then I would grab Ryan's hand and wouldn't let go until we made it home safe. I would silently pray, *"Please, God, help my dad to drive straight."* It baffles me to this day that we made it home safe, night after night.

What I picked up from my father, besides the habit of addiction, was the idea that an addiction could be the most important thing in life. His lifestyle told me that drinking and women were more important than I was. To realize this left me angry and hurt, with no way of being able to communicate how I felt. I can look back and forgive him now, because I know it was his disease that caused him to make this choice. But to a child's mind, the choice was a complete abandonment by an incompetent father. The first time that I ever tried drugs was in a situation where love was what I wanted. I fell head over heels for a drug called marijuana on a warm summer day in Colorado. It was a huge moment in my life. After I fell in love with drugs, everything changed. I did have thoughts about what I was doing. It was as if my brain would overload with memories about my father and thoughts of what would happen to me if I became a druggie. Would I become dirty, homeless, and lonely like the addicts I'd seen on TV or in the movies? Or would I become like my dad? But I never wanted to get stupid drunk and high like he would get. It bewilders me now to think that he used to take me with him to score dope.

It plays in my head like it was yesterday, as the dealer walks up to my dad's car window and hands him a bag of weed. My father even kept a scale in his car to make sure he was never ripped off. Upon returning to his apartment I would be told to play outside, while he would sit in the living room rolling joints and getting high. The women in my father's life seemed to come and go through all this. What these women had in common was the fact that they loved alcohol as much as he did. It's easy to meet a guy like Chuck, the person who gave me my first joint, or my dad, if you are interested in being addicted to their drug of choice. My father's second wife, Jen, was the spitting image of my father, as if a female version of him had been made. I think their love for alcohol was the only thing that kept them together for as long as they were.

They were also in the same line of work, construction. I can remember when my dad and Jen would come home smelling the same and looking the same, both soiled and stinky. You'd think the first thing they would want to do would be to take a shower, but that came in as a close second to their after-work beer binge. I was never close to Jen; she kind of scared me. I never felt safe around her. Even though I was young I could still see what was going on between them. They never seemed happy or sober. I'm not sure if they thought that I was too young to know what was going on or if they were too caught up in their own disease to care. Maybe it was a little of both. I dreaded when it was their weekend for my brother and I to visit. I could never be too sure what kind of mood Jen was going to be in.

Jen could be very scary to me when she wanted to be. There were times when she would chase me down the hall to catch and spank the hell out of me for fighting with my brother or touching something of hers that I was not supposed to be touching. Eventually I got smart, and I would run into my bedroom and get under the bottom bunk, where she couldn't reach me when she tried to get violent. The screaming that she did was horrible. I would lie in dog droppings under the bed to avoid her wrath, but as long as she didn't catch me, I didn't care. I would just lie there until my father came home, knowing that as soon as he arrived, Jen would act different. She never acted that way in front of him. I knew I was safe from her, for a while anyway.

I can faintly remember that they tried to get sober a couple of times together. At the time, I didn't realize what was going on, but later when I got into recovery, I understood exactly what they were doing. Instead of going to the bars, they took us to an old two-story house, where meetings were going on. I can remember playing with other kids outside the house while our parents sat inside drinking coffee, smoking cigarettes, and talking. I found all this to be quite weird because it was a completely different scene from the bars I had become used to. I finally had something in common with other children, though, which bonded me to them. None of us had been allowed to just be kids because of the addictions in our homes, but when our parents were in those meetings, they were changed for a while. Finally, we could just be kids.

Weekend visits with my father never ended up being consistent. I was just too young to understand it all. Weekend after weekend until he would relapse again, the bars didn't exist to my father. It was only this white, two-story meetinghouse. He always seemed to land himself in jail after that for drunk driving. I remember letters showing up at the house that were postmarked from county. That was how I would find out where my dad was. The letters would be filled with empty promises of recovery and words of sorrow for missing my birthday again. It became embarrassing and heartbreaking to me, but inside I kept a little belief alive that one day he would fulfill his promises and become the father that I needed. By the time I met Chuck and tried pot, it was too late for any fatherly talk my dad and I might have had. My family never really sat me down and told me about our legacy of addiction.

Truthfully, it's ironic I became an addict. In elementary school I had a counselor who was a very warm man who ran a group I was assigned to for the children of alcoholic parents. This counselor would come and pull me out of class to attend the meetings, which I thought was the coolest thing ever. I felt special and like I belonged to something that not everyone else could belong to. We would get to sit around and talk about our situation and learn how to better cope with the stress of an alcoholic parent. The counselor made us all feel comfortable sharing about our family situations, and the group provided us with a nonjudgmental environment. I felt accepted and no longer like an outcast because of my lack of a cookie cutter mom and dad and perfect home life. I didn't view the counselor as a fill-in daddy by any means; however, he was stepping in as someone who gave me the fatherly advice I never got at home.

By sixth grade I was still involved in these antiaddiction programs. DARE, the Drug Abuse Resistance Education program, was a place where I became one of the more active kids. Because of my family situation, I frowned upon drugs and alcohol in a passionate way. I wrote an essay about the various ways DARE had helped me and was asked to read it in front of the whole school. If people at school had seen me five years later, maybe they never would have believed I had become addicted to drugs. I can see now that I was passionate about being appreciated more than I was passionate about the message of DARE. I thrived on being given the opportunity to lead.

During the time I was in DARE, I found out that my dad was getting remarried. His marriage to Jen hadn't lasted. At first his new wife seemed nice, but it didn't take long to find out that she drank just as much as my dad did, if not more. I was twelve years old then. This is when Ryan and I went to stay with my dad and his new wife, Sylvia, for the summer. It only took a few weeks before I got to see her true colors. They were darker even than Jen's. While my dad worked, Sylvia stayed home with Ryan and me, and her anger would become uncontrollable, to the point of abuse. Ryan was joking around with Sylvia one day while my dad was at work, and she went into a rage. I can remember her grabbing my brother by the neck and slamming him up against the hallway wall. When I saw what was happening, I became very frightened and knew that we had to get away from her.

At first we ran for the front door, but she blocked us. I then grabbed Ryan's hand, and we ran to the back bedroom, where we barricaded ourselves in by pushing the furniture up against the door. My main goal was to protect my brother at any cost. I had to figure out how we were going to get out of the apartment. We were on the second floor, so there was no way for us to go out the window and jump. Ryan and I decided we would wait it out. When my dad got home we thought we could tell him what happened and he would protect us. While we were hiding in the room, Sylvia had been screaming through the door for us to come out. I could tell just how enraged she was, and there was no way that I was going to face her again. We could faintly hear her at one point, talking to my dad on the phone. We couldn't make out what Sylvia was saying, but the next thing I heard was the front door of the apartment open and close, leading me to believe that she had left the apartment. I heard nothing for a while, so I decided to crack the door open and peek down the hall to see if the coast was clear.

As I quietly opened the door to make a run for our escape, I looked down the hall and saw nothing. When I turned to signal to my brother to start running, something hit me in the chest and threw me back against the wall. Sylvia had rammed her way into the room. She threw me out of the way. My brother jumped onto the bed, and she followed. Sylvia stood over Ryan and proceeded to kick him in the ribs. I knew everything would be okay if we could only get out of the apartment. I grabbed my brother from beneath Sylvia, and we ran until we made it out the front door. We just kept running, and I looked back every few seconds to see if she was behind us, but she was not. All I wanted was my mom. I wanted her to come and get me and not make me go back there anymore, so I found a pay phone, made a collect call, and told her that she needed to come and get us quickly.

I started to calm down after I made that call. My mom was on her way, but while waiting by the pay phone I heard my dad screaming out my name. I turned around to see him walking toward me. I felt a sense of relief to see him, because I hadn't been able to tell him what Sylvia had done yet. I knew that he could fix the situation with her, but things went differently than I had expected. He told Ryan and I to get in the car and, to no big surprise, he drove us to a bar. When we told him our story, he told us that he didn't believe us. He was angry by this point, yelling loudly enough for everyone at the bar to hear. He said he believed Sylvia's story, which was that she did not touch us at all. He was upset that we would treat his wife so badly, and he told us she was the most important thing in his life. My father told us that he wasn't willing to let anything mess that up.

Growing up, I had wanted my dad to appreciate me, and here he was, choosing his alcohol and his addiction to a woman over the word of his own daughter about being abused. At least I had succeeded in leading Ryan to safety. When my dad became very concerned about what we were going to tell our mom, I wasn't concerned at all. I had no reason to lie about what happened. My father was telling me to keep it a secret, but I refused to give in to his desperation. My mom needed to know, and I didn't understand how my father expected me to lie. Once she picked us up I told her the story of how Sylvia had physically hurt Ryan and that we had to hide from her in the bedroom until we could get away. It was a relief that my mom had finally come for us, but I was very confused and angry. *How could this be happening* is all I could think. A dad is supposed to protect his kids, yet he had chosen to hang me out to dry. His own flesh and blood was just another casualty along the way.

It would be a year and a half before I would hear from my father again, and I started acting out around that same time. I was starved for attention. I also didn't have the coping skills I needed to go through the kinds of events caused by the addicts around me, events that were the story of my family's life. The attention I wanted came easily when I would get in trouble. I quickly realized that the attention was negative, but it was still attention, and I learned to get it from people who were safe, unlike Sylvia. Before long it became a regular act of mine to give my teachers a hard time and play the class clown. I found that other kids would egg me on. To have attention from them was such a great feeling. My beast of addiction was awakened by this harmless wish to be appreciated and loved. The acting up eventually became normal behavior for me and kept feeding into itself. It was as if I had become a ball of negative energy that was consumed with anger and hate.

As the time went by I became angrier and lonelier. In middle school my family moved across town. I was very set on making friends after the move and keeping them. I became a great actress, with the ability to mold myself to what others wanted me to be, which would be a trait that came in handy once I started using full-time. The friends I made at my new school were already experimenting with drugs, but I had no interest in participating. I smoked cigarettes, but that was all during this time, and my mom had no idea. If my friends ever asked if I had been high before, I lied and said yes. I didn't want anyone to think I was lame and inexperienced. My mom could have appreciated this, based on her own fears growing up.

Our family moved again after the end of this year, to Colorado, where I did give in to the peer pressure of drugs. That's when I met Chuck, who introduced me to pot. I was back into my lonely space after the move, without the friends I had worked so hard to make. My dad also got back in touch with me. A letter arrived in the mail after I had heard nothing from him for a year and a half, and the letter was postmarked from the Yavapai County jail, in Arizona. He was in prison for driving under the influence, which made me upset. I just wanted to be alone. It didn't seem fair that my dad was so good at vanishing from my life while other kids never had to experience this. I didn't understand why he couldn't be the father that I needed him to be. He had done everything the opposite of the way I believed a father was supposed to act. I took his letter to the side of our house to read it in private. In the letter, my dad wrote that he had made a decision to stop drinking and therefore could no longer have Sylvia in his life. He wrote that he was sorry for everything that he had done to cause me pain and that he wanted to stop hurting the people that he loved the most and become a better man and father.

He made promises that things were now going to be different. At that point, I had no reason to doubt his promises. He hadn't begun the string of arrests, letters, and promises that he would be different that I would receive from him over the next few years. And of course his message was the promise that every little girl without a father wants to hear. Somehow it seemed that he and I were a little closer to the fairytale relationship I could have only dreamed of by then. The men in my life at the time were either related to me, or they were boys I was meeting through my brother, like Chuck. At first I was absolutely shocked to find out that my brother had been smoking pot with Chuck, but the shock soon turned into curiosity, and I leaned in a little closer so I could become part of their world.

Chuck was a few years older than me, and quite a bit older than my brother. I soon found out that they shared a common bond, though. They both liked to smoke marijuana. As we all sat together the first day I chose to try drugs, Chuck reached into his jacket pocket and pulled out a pipe and a bag of weed. I played it cool on the outside, but on the inside I was completely freaking out. It was as if a great war began inside my head. Part of me knew that it was wrong, but the other part of me just couldn't say no anymore. I didn't do it because I wanted to rebel, and I didn't do it because I thought it would be fun or because I felt I had to because that was my family legacy. I made the decision to get high at that moment because I wanted to be accepted.

When Chuck and my brother gave me a chance to try pot, it became a huge moment in my life. It was a moment when I learned that I could be carefree and a moment when I learned drugs could somehow fill the void that had always been inside of me. Something that was supposed to be so terrible for me really offered feelings of euphoria, happiness, and fulfillment. I realized that pot was something great that I had been missing out on for so long. In my father's letter that year he had promised to be different. I would be different, too, because I actually became more like the addict he had been when I was growing up. I can see the scene when this happened so clearly in my mind. Chuck, Ryan, and I sat on a hill with the sun shining down on us. After I tried weed on that hill, I soon began to wonder if alcohol would also produce the same effect for me. I find this to be the power of addiction. The years I spent hating drugs and alcohol were reversed after one time taking drugs. In a matter of seconds, I lost all defenses to the beast.

This is when the illness of addiction began to take control of my life. I was the new kid in Colorado. I had trouble making friends, and I was scared to take any risks and meet new people. All the people I met there pretty much had a place where they already fit in, a crowd that they belonged to. I just couldn't seem to find my place. I was surrounded by hundreds of kids but felt like the loneliest person in the world. I dreaded each day that I had to get out of bed and face eating lunch by myself once again. To my mom, everything may have looked relatively good, other than a few calls from school that I was acting up, but on the inside I felt alone and lost, and I didn't see any point in letting her know. Things had gotten really bad at school, but I knew that she wasn't going to be able to fix that. It was up to me to find my place in our new town.

I found Chuck, eventually, and found the neighborhood friends Ryan and I shared, Christy and Danny, later on. At school all the lonely kids like me, the misfits and new kids, just kind of hung together. Deeper down we knew that if any of us could have made a better friend, we would have. I became impatient for summer to come because of that wish to get away from these nobodies. Meeting Chuck had introduced me to a whole different world that had opened the door to me if I was willing to live like an addict, and by that time I was. I became an addict that first day I lit up. In no time at all, I was looking for my second and third high. I had to have more. I had to reach the high that I experienced the first time, and it became my quest to feel okay. After feeling fine for the first time in my life, I never wanted to go back to feeling insecure. I wasn't afraid to talk to people when I was high. I didn't wish I were someone else. I never wanted to reverse that effect.

Within a couple of weeks I developed strep throat because I was using so frequently. As I sat in the doctor's office, I was sure I would have to submit a urine sample and my pot smoking would be found out. This was my introduction to the paranoia that is a side effect of addiction. Paranoia is the constant companion of the addict. The nurse at the office noticed I had dropped seventeen pounds in a two-week period, but she hadn't asked for a sample. She talked about my weight instead, and as far as I could remember I hadn't stopped eating, so I didn't have an answer. My mom and I never discussed it further; we just left it as a mystery, maybe a temporary part of the adjustment to our move, which we didn't try to overanalyze. I had figured that if anything I had gained weight, from overeating when I had the munchies after smoking pot.

Then the nurse eventually did ask for the urine sample, and my heart dropped to the floor. This was it for me, obviously. I could tell I was going to be busted for sure. Again, this was paranoia. The nurse had asked for the urine sample because she wanted to rule out the possibility I had developed diabetes, which might have accounted for the rapid change in my weight. My mom had no clue about my drug use when we were at this appointment. She could have asked the nurse to run the urine tests for drugs, but why would she? She only had a sense that something was different with me after we moved to Colorado. That summer I tried my best to reach my next drunk or high. Maybe it would have turned out differently if my mom had followed her instinct that I was different and assumed I was using drugs, because I was, but I wasn't so different she couldn't recognize me. I looked a lot like she had looked at my age. I began to isolate myself, lie, and steal. I also let my addiction become the most important thing in my life, just like my dad did.

THE PROGRESSION
OF THE DISEASE

CHAPTER 8

IT SEEMED AS IF I had started a whole new life for myself. It didn't
come easy to stay high, though, because I hardly knew anybody
besides Chuck and the other kids Ryan knew that did drugs. I had
to persuade one of these people to steal alcohol for me at the beginning, because I was always too chicken to steal it from the grocery
store myself. It became evident early on that I would have to get brave
enough to use my own acting skills to stay high as often as I needed
to. I needed to become a great manipulator and liar. My summer had
led into the first year at high school, where again I had no friends.
This is when I met Ryan's friend, Danny, and his sister, Christy. I
struck up a conversation almost instantly with Danny about our

mutual interest in getting high. It was just like my dad and Jen had been with their alcohol, or Chuck and I had been with our pot. I gathered from the way Danny explained his habit that he just might be the connection and friend I had been waiting for.

We walked miles on the afternoon I met him to find Christy, because she supposedly hung out where we could buy some pot. I'd never purchased drugs before, but I was ready. I was excited to have my very first and very own bag of weed. Christy went to the same school that I did and was in my grade, so as I walked up to the place where I first met her, I sensed I was about to meet a good friend. At school the next day I stumbled upon her again, and her friends were all gathered together during lunch. She recognized me and asked me if I wanted to hang out. The feeling was wonderful. I was in complete awe of Christy and thought her friends were all beautiful and seemed so much more experienced than I was with drugs. Because we all shared a connection with drugs, it was as if I was instantly accepted. After meeting these girls, I always had someone to get high with and to walk home with me. Christy and Danny lived one street over from our house in Colorado. She and I soon became very close friends and did everything together, and it didn't take long before getting high together became an everyday occurrence.

I soon figured out that in the world of addiction, the person with the drugs is the person with all the power. Everyone is instantly this person's best friend, which was the kind of attention I had always craved. When I realized this was the way it worked, I was willing to do whatever it took to keep experiencing the highs of my new world. My allowance wasn't enough to support my mari-juana and alcohol use by then, so I started sneaking out at night to break into the neighborhood cars to look for any valuables or money I could scrounge up. To my surprise, lots of people didn't lock their car doors. Sometimes I would find money, and sometimes I would take clothes or expensive jackets that I could then sell to friends for drugs. Acid became an option, but I resisted at first. Somehow my mind had convinced me that I was still in control of myself as long as I didn't take it past alcohol and pot. Acid made me rethink my opinion. I was surprised that all I had to do was put a little white square of paper on my tongue to get high from LSD.

Each time I tried a new drug, I liked it better than the last. I didn't have control of my addiction, no matter what I believed. Alcohol and pot were a part of my everyday life, and I added LSD on the weekends. I had no clue that my mom had compromised with her drug use the same way I was beginning to. Both of us were "weekend warriors" in our own ways. Being on drugs like this gradu-ally became an easy and comfortable way for me to live. Through friends of my brother I met new drug connections, like Larry and his wife, Annie, who lived on the street behind me. Larry was twenty-six and fed me a constant supply of drugs and alcohol and gave all the neighborhood kids a place to party. No more standing outside in Colorado blizzards, freezing and soaking myself just to get high without my mom catching me. Larry liked me instantly. He invited me to his house any time I wanted to party. It didn't take long before I took his offer and brought Christy to meet him, and we were showing up at Larry's every day after school.

I was having so much fun living this way, and I wasn't going to let anything or anyone get in my way. Getting high was more important than anything else. There was no room for family, chores, or schoolwork. It was obvious to my mom that I had changed. She was baffled as to why, partly because she had no proof I was using and partly because of her own denial, which kept her from looking for the clues that she could have seen, like my weight loss. She would come home and find that my chores weren't done or have to take calls from my teachers, who confronted her about my continuously missing schoolwork. The only way that I really knew how to react was to be argumentative. It was as if I had started building a wall around myself made of pure anger. It fought off anyone who came too close. The anger wasn't hard to keep alive because I lived in fear that my secret would be found out, and I was willing to do anything to protect it. I was skipping class with my friends. They didn't usually end up going back to school after ditching to get high, so I would just follow them, and wherever they ended up, I ended up.

It became a game to sneak off campus and run from the school supervisors that drove around the grounds in golf carts, acting like a fleet of police. They knew through the grapevine that other kids came looking to me for dope. Because of this suspicion, any time a supervisor felt like it, I was searched. Occasionally, the supervisors would catch me on the Path, a jumble of trees across the street from my school where everyone who wanted to smoke cigarettes or get high would hide. It was pretty obvious that you were hiding something if a supervisor caught you on the Path. The only reason kids went there was to do things that weren't allowed. One of the closest calls on the Path I can remember was with Christy. The campus supervisors came roaring over in the golf carts on a witch hunt for us, just as soon as we had lit the cigarettes we always smoked to cover up the smell after we smoked pot.

We weren't the only people on the Path that day, so the supervisors began to round everyone up. When they had, they barked marching orders for us to return to class. I thought Christy and I had blended in with everyone else and made a close escape, but just before we were out of sight, the supervisors told us to follow them to the main office at school. I thought they were going to bust us for ditching, or write us up for being off campus at worst. To my surprise they asked me to empty my pockets. They never found anything on me, and Christy came up clean, too, because she had been smart enough to hide her pipe in her bra. They couldn't nail us, but they made it clear that the smell of the marijuana was very heavily on us. They told us it would only be a matter of time before we would finally be caught red-handed. I ended up at Larry's house after that, only that time I arrived to find somebody new at his house. Larry kept a tight circle of people around him because of the fear. It wasn't very often that someone new came around.

Addiction makes you fearful that your secret will get out. If the secret gets out, you get busted, which means the addiction can't continue, and that's worse than being caught red-handed. Nothing could be worse for an addict than being forced to stop. All of us worried constantly about the people we opened up to. An addict has to limit the people he or she knows to ensure the secret of addiction stays safe. Larry had a huge secret. He had purchased four hundred dollars' worth of cocaine from the new person hanging around. They asked me if I wanted to stay and party, so I said yes and quickly found a spot to sit on the floor. I did four and half lines and didn't leave that spot for the next five hours. I just sat there numb, observing all the conversation around me. I felt like I was having an out-of-body experience, and I loved every second of it. PCP, a drug called phencyclidine, came next. I began to smoke marijuana laced with the stuff and catch the feelings of strength, power, and invulnerability PCP gives. I spent the next two months on a constant high of marijuana, alcohol, acid, cocaine, and PCP.

To stay high all day, every day, I opened myself up to dabbling in anything and everything I could get my hands on. I was failing all my classes at school because I had missed so many days. When I would show up at all, it was just to get my mom off my back. She yelled at me sometimes. She didn't know what else to do but get mad about the changes she could see in me. Going to school was something I could do that made it seem normal for both of us, so I did it sometimes to make her feel okay, but then the drugs would consume me again and crumble this facade I was trying to manage for my mom and me. One particular day that I went to school, the group of girls that I hung out with decided to fight a girl we didn't like. I took such pleasure in the power we had to terrify this girl. Because of my threats, the school had called my house, and the police followed Christy and I home to make sure this girl would be safe from us. I wasn't doing a good job at making anything normal by doing things like that. I decided that I wouldn't go home that night and that it was better if I just ran away. Christy and I were going to leave together. We wanted to be free to party and have no one around to tell us that we had to stop.

We had no money to make it on our own. It was Christy's idea to steal money from her parents for us to get started with our plan, but her parents kept their bedroom door locked. They knew Christy could not be trusted. Money and valuables had already come up missing from their home. There were obvious indications all around us that people distrusted us and that we weren't welcome. Christy decided that it didn't matter. She was going to break in no matter what it took to steal her parents' money, so I waited down at the end of the street for her to show up. I wasn't sure if she would, but sure enough Christy came running, carrying a big tin full of coins. Once I saw that we had only a few dollars' worth of change, I started to rethink our running away idea. Quarters weren't going to get us very far. Christy explained to me though that to get the loot she had to beat the door with a bathroom plunger, that the door was destroyed, and that she wasn't going back no matter what. To hang in there with my friend, I had to keep on with our plan.

We spent the next couple of days getting high on anything we could get our hands on. A close friend of ours, Carrie, invited us to her brother's place to party and stay the night. The whole time I was there I had knots in my stomach. I just wanted to consume as much alcohol and drugs as I could so that I wouldn't have to feel so horrible anymore. I knew that my family was worried sick about me, but I just wanted to keep getting high, even if hurting them was the cost. This was when Ryan told me that if my mom found me I was headed for inpatient, because she had been searching for me frantically with Christy's mom. Things were really starting to get scary at this point. I wondered where I was going to go if I really couldn't go home anymore. I had always been able to figure a way out of bad situations that my addictions led me into. My mom outsmarted me on this one, tracked me down at Carrie's brother's house, and put me in her car. I was on my way to the mental hospital after that, and she wouldn't stop for anything, no matter how much I tried to lie about needing to use the restroom or manipulate her into stopping to buy cigarettes to calm me down.

I felt completely beaten. My mom was acting different. She was very bold, and it seemed like I was becoming weak. What had happened to me could not be dealt with inside my head, or with drugs, and I was too out of control to even think of other options. At the hospital after my mom had checked me in I felt like my world came crashing down. I was told I couldn't go home. I was searched. A staff member took away my shoelaces, even, for fear that I would try to hang myself with them. I was put in a cold room that had only one window covered by bars, which made me feel like a prisoner in a scary place. It was no vacation, I realized, sitting there alone without my drugs or my friends or even my mom. The other patients were all kids around my age, but they were different from me. Many were violent on occasion, and some didn't talk at all as a result of being mentally ill. All I could think was that this hospital was not a safe place to make friends. I was stuck with a bunch of weirdos and freaks.

The staff didn't know what to do with me, or how to help. The people around me weren't there for drugs, like I was, so I got the impression the doctors didn't understand me, and if they couldn't understand me I didn't believe they could reach me. I told my doctor what he wanted to hear, just so he would let me go home. I figured that if I followed the rules and did everything my doctor said, I would get out pretty fast. While I was lying to gain my freedom, all the other patients were being given doses of medication. The nurse would attentively watch these patients, one by one, to make sure they actually took the pills. The kids were so doped up that some couldn't even talk, and when they did talk, they would drool all over as if they had no control. One of the girls even had to have Vaseline put on her face because the medication she was given had made her skin peel off.

I lived watching scenes like that for nine days before I was allowed to check out. All I could think of was the fact that I didn't belong in that hospital. But then I had to ask how I had ended up there and couldn't come up with an answer. I was in total denial. I was healthy compared to the other patients, but I had lost any ability to notice the fact that my family's beast had totally consumed me and taken over my life. I had no control of my addictions. After I was released from the hospital, I was sent to stay with my grandparents in Montana, where the lifestyle I had known was unavailable. I didn't meet any friends that used, so I had nothing better to do than watch TV. That became an addiction, too. I obsessively and continuously watched MTV all day long. The celebrities and the clothes in the music videos made me feel surer than ever there was something wrong with me without my drugs. The fact was, I felt inadequate in life. My mom thought I looked happy in the pictures she saw of me during this time. If only she had known.

I'd have thought that after feeling so low in Montana I could have figured out the emotions I had experienced were signs that things in my life needed to change. But the fact is that as soon as I got back to my old stomping grounds, I started up where I had left off and got high. I realized after I returned that I had missed out on so much partying. I wanted to start making up for lost time, so I met up with old friends immediately and resumed my old behavior. I justified my using with the conclusion that I didn't want to look stupid anymore. Montana had been enough. I wanted to feel better than I had watching MTV, and as good as people on that channel looked on the outside. By then I had plenty of justifications for using alcohol and drugs. It was easy to use one or another of them to deny the downward spiral I was in, which wasn't letting up emotionally. I had no idea how to deal with real pain or feelings. I didn't know how to deal with fear. Using became so important to me because it seemed to dissolve all the fear I had. It's an emotional exchange for an addict, because getting high will take you from complete and total despair to greatness in a matter of minutes. I had given drugs and alcohol the responsibility to fill all my voids by this time in my life.

Christy and I took off again after I returned home, and this time we stayed gone for a five-day, constant high. I'd had plenty of time to think about things while I was locked up in the hospital. I realized that what I needed was to get better about hiding my drugs so that I could continue with my addictions. I was going to have to make everything look good on the outside, which included staying home more often, acting like I was interested in family activities, returning to school, actually going to my classes, and doing my homework. I kept this up for the first two months of my sophomore year before I was thrown out of school, big surprise, for having drugs.

The reason my disease is a disease is that it tells me it is not a disease, which is why I continued to believe I could follow through with plans to seem normal while living the life of an addict. My mom would always find my stash eventually. I would be so careful to hide my using, but then I would end up leaving evidence lying around because I didn't think straight while I was high. I couldn't follow through or remember plans. There were also times when my mom sneaked behind my back. She and I were locked in a battle of lies against Tough Love techniques. I would search for hours in our house if I believed I had misplaced my drugs. The fact was, she had flushed them down the toilet and decided not to tell me. By the time I heard the news I would have completely torn my room apart in panic, paranoia, and fear.

When my mother's choices forced me to admit I was an addict, I just lied to the counselors she tried to bring in to help me and said I wanted to change, or just flat-out told them I refused to quit. Ryan and I were kicked out of school often in those days, so it became easy to party every day at our house, no matter how many boundaries my mom tried to set down. She had to go to work, so we would wait, and after she left our friends would show up to get high. I thought it was the coolest thing ever that my friends were at school and I got to stay home and do nothing all day. The only thing that sometimes dragged me down was a huge knot in my gut. I knew I was hurting my family. I felt like the only way I could make my mother happy was to quit using drugs and alcohol altogether; however, I had come to the point that I could not picture my life without them anymore. It was clear that all my wrong behavior was breaking her down. She was a single parent just trying to do the best she could, and I was taking complete advantage of her.

The drug parties at our house stopped when Ryan and I were admitted into our first drug rehab, as another consequence of my mother's Tough Love techniques. It was another hospital, with all the same crazies I had seen before, but at least they had been assigned to a separate floor. The doctor I was assigned was an identical match to good old Santa Claus, a fact about him that I took for a joke. I was fifteen years old; I took nothing seriously at the time, and I made sure it stayed that way by getting high every morning before the recovery program began and every day after, when I would return home. I was sent into a panic when I learned that Santa Claus planned to drug-test me a couple of times a week. How was I going to get away with using now? He mentioned that for a while my drug tests would come up dirty. Ah, I thought, a loophole. I could still get high. I just had to keep decreasing my use to make it seem like the drugs were slowly leaving my system.

Each test began to come back, showing that I had less and less drugs in my system, until one test came back showing very high levels of marijuana. I was busted and had to admit to myself that my plan had failed. There was no way around this one, because I had to face the evidence this time. But I still figured I could work around the problem. I thought if I was just more honest with Santa Claus, it would get him off my back, and he would feel like the job he was doing was paying off. The next week I carelessly kept getting high. Trying to pass the test by drinking tons of water and quitting for a bit, a few days before, didn't help. My test came back positive again, and I was drilled about my drug use. I made all these attempts to get around the system because I couldn't even fathom what it would be like to stop using drugs. In fact, being addicted was all I felt I was good at. I feared that if I didn't have the drugs and alcohol anymore, I would have absolutely no identity at all.

In times of desperation, my need to protect this identity always got more extreme. I knew that I couldn't fail one more drug test with Santa Claus, but quitting wasn't an option either. I thought long and hard about ways I could work around this dilemma, and I came to the conclusion that I would focus on the kinds of drugs I heard did not stay in a person's system for long. I had heard LSD did not stay in the system, and because I had access to acid it seemed like a logical solution. This is how my addiction always advanced. I would try a new drug because it was available, or because it solved a problem I had that threatened the life I had created. Soon after taking LSD, everything in my life revolved around a little tiny paper square. I took using acid to the extreme. At this time I was sleeping down in the basement of our house, where black lights and black light posters surrounded me. Rainbows of colors decorated my walls, sheets, blankets, and even my Slinky. It gave me extreme visual effects and made everyone who dropped acid in my room feel like we had landed on a different planet.

Acid didn't show up in my drug tests, so I took it one step further after hearing that good news. I began to smuggle LSD into the recovery program, to sell hits to other patients for more than I bought the drugs for. The money I made went to paying for me to continue using. By this time my mom had cut off the money. She knew that it would have been spent on drugs. This was also when my alcohol consumption increased. I had heard that alcohol left the system very fast, so it became something for me to always fall back on. Liquor was easy to find and very affordable. The only thing that was necessary to manage at this point was selecting the right drug for my schedule. A normal LSD trip lasts twelve to eighteen hours. That had to be saved for days that Ryan and I did not have to attend our recovery program. The better option was to smoke pot before or after our program at the hospital, which we did. I found comfort in the fact that my brother was going through all this with me. We were two peas in a pod. If I had drugs I got Ryan high, and if he had drugs he got me high, and one of us was always bound to have something.

The approach to addiction at our recovery program was to try and scare the addictions out of us by using statistical charts and graphs and a bunch of useless facts that we cared nothing about. We were even asked to climb poles with the help of others and scale walls, like rock climbers, as a way to learn trust for others, as if trust were the key to getting us off drugs. A fear of experiencing pain or the inability to know how to feel real emotions and then work through difficult things keeps a person addicted. All the rehab program ended up becoming to me was a place where I was able to sit around and try to top the war stories I heard from other addicts.

I didn't know or care that after our move to Arizona my addiction would go from bad to worse. I just knew that I wasn't done making a life for myself in Colorado when my mom announced that we were moving back to Phoenix. I had made so many friends by that time that I did not want to leave. Everyone I knew helped me focus on my addictions. To make sure my life would remain the same after I moved, I quickly made a couple of phone calls to friends in Arizona. I had kept in touch with a few people who had access to anything that I might want or need after I got to town.

FROM BAD TO WORSE

CHAPTER 9

Upon arriving in Arizona, I moved in with my godmother, Mary, while my mother handled the move and looked for a house to buy. I was not opposed to this because my godmother was very lenient concerning what I did, where I went, and what time I returned home. Her big mistake was to have trusted me. After I moved in I completely took advantage of the fact that she gave me plenty of freedom to do as I wished. She wanted to believe so badly that I was a good kid. I wanted to believe that, too, but I wasn't ready to make that step. I called her nephew, Steve, who had been my best friend since the age of three. As soon as I met up with him, my life became a 24-7 party because he was using and had an entire circle of friends and family that also used. We grew up together but had still kept in touch when I lived in Colorado. We would chat here and there on the phone about the types of drugs we had experimented with. It was only natural that I contact him as soon as I got to Arizona because he offered me friendship I didn't have anywhere else right after the move and shared a lifestyle in which it wasn't a problem to make addiction the most important thing.

At first he would sneak us his mother's alcohol by pouring it into closed containers so that no one would be the wiser that he was stealing it. We would sit in his room getting drunk on that and smoking weed. Many nights I would be too drunk to go home, so I would just call Mary and let her know I would be staying the night at her nephew's house. It was the perfect situation to party all night long and have absolutely no consequences except a hangover. Quickly, I became very happy in this situation because I was able to stay intoxicated around the clock and couldn't feel much else besides the high. I bragged to Ryan about it. I told my brother he was missing out on so much because he had chosen to live with our dad, way out in Cottonwood. I may not have landed at Mary's without Ryan living with my dad instead of my mom. She desperately wanted us both away from the drugs in Colorado, so she had let him go as soon as he wanted to leave for Cottonwood. I ended up at Mary's house because my mom had to finish up her last week of work and wanted me out of Colorado, too. Ryan would come down to Phoenix for weekend visits. When he did we headed over to Steve's house to party, so Ryan could see what I had been telling him. He couldn't believe we were able to party, right there in the house, with Steve's mother home and just down the hall.

Steve lived in a family of people who partied. They didn't have a problem with the way we partied because they partied, too. His mom and aunt were very heavy drinkers, and because of that there was a constant supply of beer and hard liquor at Steve's house. It was normal to see his mother with a beer in her hand. There never needed to be a special occasion to celebrate with a drink because it was just an everyday occurrence. On a weekend visit to Steve's with Ryan, he mentioned he had brought money with him to the house and wanted to know if Steve could find him a bag of weed. Easily done, and to our surprise we were able to buy the pot from one of Steve's family members, his older cousin, Bert. This guy seemed very skeptical about supplying us with the weed at first, so Steve had to convince him Ryan and I weren't new to pot, and that we knew what we were doing. In the end Bert wound up being very generous with the drugs.

If it wasn't enough for Ryan to believe we could buy drugs from Steve's family members, we went to the back yard with our weed to get high after our buy. I can remember freaking out because Steve's whole family was over for a barbeque on that day. There we were, standing in the back yard, out in the open in front of all these strangers, smoking a bowl. But Steve kept assuring me that it was okay, and the next thing I knew Steve's mother came walking up behind us like it wasn't. My stomach curled up into knots when she called Steve over. Instantly my brain started working in overtime to find a way out if we were busted. My paranoia always had me rehearsing what I would say, or thinking about what excuses I could come up with. I felt sick as the adrenaline was pumping through my veins. I said to myself, *Here we go again.* How had I ended up in a situation where I was about to get busted for drugs? The answer was that I hadn't ended up in a situation like that. Steve's mom walked over to us and asked if she could take a hit.

I was in complete shock, yet relieved at the same time, when this occurred. This was a major discovery about the way life could be for me from then on, and I knew it was going to take some time for my brain to work the entire situation out. It really couldn't get any better for a fifteen-year-old drug addict. A world of opportunity had opened up for me, and I continued to be a regular guest at Steve's house. A normal day would consist of watching TV and getting high with Steve, his mother, and his aunt. This was just their way of life, but to me it was a dream. Any time I wanted to get high I just went to his house, and if I partied too hard, I didn't have to go home. I learned how the system at Steve's worked after sticking around awhile. His aunt bought a quarter pound of weed weekly, just for home use. If we ran out early, we would just scrape all the bongs and paraphernalia in the house for residue, which would produce mounds of pot residue as big as a paper plate. If the platefuls weren't an option, there was always my good old friend alcohol. It was always there at Steve's house and always free.

By my sixteenth birthday, this is the list of drugs I used constantly: massive amounts of marijuana, LSD, mushrooms, PCP, cocaine, and alcohol. A couple of days after my sixteenth birthday, I tried crystal meth for the first time. The night I did, I didn't have much else to do. I can't recall why I wasn't at Steve's house that night, but it didn't stop me from my search for the next high. Bored, fidgety, and sober at Mary's, I decided to go for a walk up to the corner store. Mind you the neighborhood surrounding her house wasn't the best. I felt absolutely invincible when I started in on a plan to get high, so I didn't care about that. When I began walking home I heard someone calling for me. There were a couple of guys standing behind the store who had yelled. They were obviously selling some kind of drugs and were waving me over to them. At first I wasn't going to stop, but a voice inside my head reminded me I hadn't found my high yet and I was still sober. I figured these guys might just be my chance to change that.

Before I knew it I was with three strange men on the stairs at their apartment building, sitting outside their apartment door. I knew it was a matter of time before they were going to let me get high. It was a game to watch them, as each guy tried to stake his claim on me. None of them had any chance. I just wanted the guys for their drugs. It was finally the oldest guy who invited me into the apartment and quickly pulled out a bag. It was full of white powder. I assumed it was cocaine in the sack until I sniffed my first line. It was instantly obvious that I had snorted something different. I asked the guy what it was I had taken, and before he told me, he just looked at me as if I were kidding, so I had to sit there and wait for his response, secretly freaking out. I didn't know what I had just inhaled into my nose. He finally blared, "Crystal meth!"

At the point I discovered I had just done crystal meth, I wanted to disappear forever. It was as if I could hear my heart breaking inside of me. Any self-worth that I did have left at that point just faded away. I had never thought that I could stoop so low. Meth was always the one thing that I said I never wanted to get into. I had known people that had gotten caught up in it, and I saw them begin to deteriorate with my very own eyes. It was like watching someone slowly die in front of you, to watch an addict on crystal meth, but the person would continue to act like nothing had changed. Seeing that had made me think that I was always going to be smarter than those people were, and I was never going to get hooked on meth. Now I know my mother made deals in a similar way with the drugs she allowed herself to use. I can relate to the feeling of believing you are smarter than a different addict. My mom felt smarter than my dad and the users he brought around their house because she believed she had more self-control than they did, and she didn't stoop to the level of using IV drugs when that became their thing.

I didn't stick around the apartment very long after discovering what I had done to myself. The guys could tell I was anxious to leave and let me know that if I decided that I wanted more meth, no problem. They told me I could come back anytime and get high for free or have the drugs at an extremely generous rate. I scurried out of the place as fast as I could, but the meth had kicked in extremely fast. Before I knew it I was higher than I had ever been, so by the time I got back to my godmother's house, I felt my heart racing and my eyes pushing hard to jump out of my head. I sat on the couch and could not stop tapping my foot on the floor. I became worried that Mary was going to notice all of this. I decided to tell her good night and headed off to my room. Little did I know that meth makes it impossible to sleep. I just lay there in bed tossing and turning. I stared at the ceiling for eight straight hours.

Each minute that passed felt like an hour that night. In the dark room by myself, my head continued to spin. I could not stop my brain from going a mile a minute. Crystal meth is an amphetamine, a drug that speeds up your head to make energy and euphoria explode in bursts. I loved this sensation more than anything that I had ever known in my whole existence. That compromise I had made with myself to never stoop so low as to try meth had all but disappeared, and so did any worry that I couldn't stop my toes from tapping uncontrollably or find a way to get any sleep. That next morning I got ready for my day in record time, the meth still cheering me on. I had so much energy, and I could accomplish so much high on it. The first thing I did was call Steve. I told him about my night, and it just seemed to make his day when I told him that I knew where to score more of it for very cheap. Within hours we were sitting in his room getting high. I couldn't believe how high I had gotten in just a matter of minutes. It confirmed I had found my miracle drug.

I was dating Robert when I began using meth. It was an on-again, off-again relationship with him. I was attracted to him not for his looks, but for his reputation within the drug dealing community. He had that attention I realized people got when they were the go-to guys or girls. I liked Robert's ability to get me high on a regular basis, and he made me feel taken care of. He always made sure to save just enough for me of anything he had on hand. Back then I found that to be romantic. He was a big guy who made me feel safe and protected. My beast was a scary, controlling thing that led me into many scary situations with many scary people, so I found great comfort in the fact that I could call Robert anytime and know he'd be there for me.

I visited him after school on a regular basis. He was nineteen or twenty at the time we dated. He rarely held a regular job because he ran with gangs and brought in the money he needed by selling drugs. I was often with him in the car when he would rob mini marts for beer. It was all pretty convenient for me until I found out that he was the superjealous type. Robert didn't care about Steve, but he didn't like the fact that I became friends with Sean, a guy from my school. Sean frequently gave me a ride home, or we would just hang out and get high. Robert didn't like it at all. He constantly grilled me, and he was always checking to see if I was staying faithful. It was mentally taxing to have a person put so little trust in me because I was obviously devoted to Robert. He was the one with the drugs, besides. So after a while all the accusations just made me frustrated. I didn't want to fight about things or talk about our emotions. I just wanted to get high.

It became apparent after a while with Sean that he had developed feelings for me. He tried to convince me to stop seeing Robert, but that wasn't an option because I needed Robert too much. I was wrapped around his little finger. For me to keep using, Robert knew he could put himself in front of me and dangle his advantage as if dangling a carrot in front of a rabbit. It didn't take long for Robert to let Sean know this directly. Robert came down the driveway with his chest all puffed up one day when Sean had dropped me off. Robert started screaming he would kill Sean if he didn't let me be. It was seconds later that Robert almost put me through a brick wall while we stood outside his house. This was followed by bouts of crying and Robert begging for my forgiveness. The contrast was confusing and scary. The behavior he was displaying was all too reminiscent of my relationships with my stepmothers. It turned me back into that frightened little girl that I hated to be.

That day distanced me from Robert. I stopped answering his calls and stopped going to his house every day. I shifted to hanging out with his uncle Lenny instead. He lived right across the street from Steve's house anyway, and although Lenny was considerably older than me, I made my way into his circle. I was sixteen and he was thirty. I wasn't naive about who Lenny was. I knew about his reputation as a big-time meth user, so if Robert was going to be violent to me, I decided I could go to Lenny instead to get high. The first night I really partied with him I had been at Steve's place first. We decided that we wanted to score meth, and the one thing you could count on with Lenny was the fact that he had it. He was always spun out. It wasn't odd to see him out in front of his house at odd hours of the morning just standing there watering his lawn. Steve and I walked over and approached Lenny, who told us we could get high around back, where he kept a shed.

The shed was out of sight. Lenny had to show us what to do that day, because he had meth for Steve and me, but we had to learn how to smoke it instead of snort it. If snorting meth was stooping low, smoking it out of a glass pipe was even lower. I knew when I was smoking it that my drug use was out of control. Every time I took a hit, it was chiseling away at who I was. I could feel my brain cells disappearing, but I didn't care. I was in love with smoking crystal meth, and just like every other first time I had with any drug, I was hooked the first time I smoked meth from the pipe. Every other drug became secondary, and I quickly learned I could also drink endless amounts of alcohol and never get sick when I used in this way. I stayed up all night, drank with everyone else, and didn't pass out or have to throw up. At that pace I actually needed the speed of meth just to keep up. Everything had to revolve around how I was going to obtain more.

At first I could buy it for myself because my mom had returned to paying me for housework. I was keeping as much as I could of my "normal routine" together for her benefit. I'd asked her to enroll me at a charter school in Phoenix when we moved back and went to class for a while and got okay grades. She didn't mind Robert but never did like him. I still saw him sometimes and used him to get free drugs when he had some meth on hand, but his uncle Lenny was always easier to find and closer to Steve's house. My mom had no problem with Steve. While I would be at Lenny's house, he would offer to get me spun out quite often. At first Steve stuck by my side when I went to Lenny's house, but later Lenny started inviting only me. I thought, *Hey, more for me,* so I didn't care. People at Steve's house started noticing I had begun disappearing. In fact, Steve's mom didn't like it too much because she knew what was going on.

Rationalizing where to draw a boundary is a way that a user can feel good about staying addicted. Somebody is always "worse off," or "past the line," but it is not you. Although I got high with Steve's mom on a regular basis, we never did meth together. That's not to say that she never used it herself, just that when she did it I was never involved. Why she set her boundary there I will never know, because everything else seemed to be acceptable in her house. The fact that she wouldn't do meth with a sixteen-year-old kid probably made her feel like she was doing a good thing for me. I didn't feel sixteen. I was used to flirting with grown men like Lenny to get a lot of free drugs when I was an addict. I learned I could get what I wanted out of them by acting a certain way. I used flirting to my advantage in Lenny's case. I milked him for as much as I could get of his meth. He delivered as much as I wanted whenever I wanted, but of course manipulation was involved. He was the one who had the upper hand, in reality, because Lenny was the one who had the drugs.

The charter school where my mom had enrolled me made my daily trips to Lenny's house, and staying high, easy to do. My school day was only four hours long, which left me the rest of the day to do as I pleased. Most of the time I would take the bus over to Lenny's after school and get a pick-me-up high before going home. Later in the night he would ride his bike the eight miles from his house over to mine, and I would sneak him in my window. I moved out of Mary's house when my mom bought a house near Shirley, the friend of hers who was encouraging my mom to keep learning Tough Love techniques and enforcing consequences against me. I'm sure I would have had more consequences if my mother knew that Lenny would usually hang out all night in my bedroom while she slept down the

hall. He stayed until just before her alarm would go off. I kept a
close eye on the clock because I knew when my mother would wake
up for work. Spun out on meth, I didn't have to sleep; therefore,
I would just start getting ready for the day like I usually would do
without my mom being any wiser.

My mom was completely oblivious of my crystal meth use,
except to notice that I got really into cleaning or a different kind
of late night task sometimes. She would have had no reason just
from seeing that to get up and check on me in the night to be sure
a guy like Lenny wasn't staying in my bedroom. My normal routine for her was going great. To her, I looked successful when I was
on meth. I was able to concentrate better and get so much more
work done than I had when I was stoned or drunk. It became routine for me to attend school without sleeping for days. If I started
coming down, I would just go to the restroom and do a line on the
top of the toilet lid to make it through the rest of the day, until I
could get back over to Lenny's house. Like Robert, Lenny always
kept enough drugs around to keep me high. He would always leave
me with enough to make it through the day, or enough to make
it until the next time that I would see him again. Eventually I cut
him out of the picture, though, when I realized there would be
more drugs for me if I didn't have to share with him. Things took
a step further toward my bottom when I chose to start getting
high by myself, but I still couldn't stop, and I didn't care.

An addict knows the behavior is destructive. I started becoming
absolutely disgusted with myself each time I realized how low I would
stoop for a high. This self-consciousness didn't escape me, even when

the beast was at its worst. I can remember standing in front of my bathroom mirror looking at myself as I made my lines to snort and noticing that I could see my skeleton through my skin. My mother had taken the door off my room in one of her Tough Love stands, so I had been left to get high in the bathroom. I was disgusting to look at, my skin was pale and gray and I had black circles under my eyes. I was saddened by the mess I had become. I couldn't stand to watch myself do one more line in the mirror, so I decided to put the rest in my pipe and smoke it with the lights off, because at least then I wouldn't have to look at myself. As I sat in the dark smoking my meth, the tears just streamed down my face. I knew I was licked, I knew I was sick, and I wasn't sure what was going to happen next.

Shirley's daughter, Lindsey, came over to party after that. She had recently been turned on to meth as well but was nowhere near the depths of my use. To my surprise, she began to tell me that she was worried about me and about how much I was using. I was shocked to be treated like such a junkie, despite what I had just seen in the mirror the night before she came over. I quickly turned the tables on Lindsey, telling her that she had no room to talk because she was also using meth. Maybe she was just jealous, I thought, because I had more dope than she did. I couldn't figure out a different reason she would be turning against me because there was no way I was ready to believe Lindsey really thought I was going to die. I didn't believe that yet, or if I did, I wasn't ready to consider it. I made plans to meet up with Lenny after I saw Lindsey. It was absolutely necessary for me to get high because I had already started coming down, Lindsey had riled me up, and I was out of my own stash.

All night I waited and waited for Lenny, looking out my blinds every three seconds for him to arrive on his bike. I was freaking out and felt sick. When he never showed, I began to make phone calls to find out where he had been. I wasn't speaking to Robert any longer, but because he was Lenny's nephew I figured I could make an exception to find out if he knew where Lenny had gone. I was devastated when I found out the police had picked him up while he was on his way over to my house. Robert let me know that Lenny would be in prison for a very long time. Apparently he had been searched and the police found a sawed-off shotgun on him and a large amount of crystal meth along with different forms of drug paraphernalia. What Lenny was doing with a sawed-off shotgun I will never know, and that is probably for the best. In fact, it was for the best, because I was forced to come down from my high that night when Lenny never showed. For the first time in a long time, I was able to feel something. I hit my bottom and had to experience how uncomfortable it was to be there.

The next few days after Lenny was arrested were absolute hell. I had no more drugs. I was terribly sick. It caused me to experience the shakes that come with drug withdrawal, and I couldn't stop dry heaving and could barely get out of bed. I slept hour upon hour. When I finally had enough strength to come out of my room, I made my way to the couch just in time to have my mom come home and confront me about my meth use. Lindsey hadn't just come over and talked to me. She had ratted me out to my mom, and I just couldn't believe it. At first I tried to convince myself that Lindsey would never do that to me. It was an unspoken rule between drug users that you just don't rat out your friends. Apparently, though, my using had scared her so much she thought I was going to die. She told her mother, who hadn't wasted any time telling my mother, who then wasted no time at all before she confronted me.

There I was sitting on our couch at home, coming off a high and in withdrawal, rattled by the news Lenny had been picked up by police and was packing a shotgun, in addition to being frustrated by Lindsey's confrontation, and then I got busted by my mom. Talk about finally feeling my bottom. My mom confronted me with the option to either go to an intake at yet another recovery program or leave her house. I didn't know if this was as bad as it got for somebody like me or if things were still going to get worse, but I knew I had to make a choice. My mom had taken her Tough Love to the harshest place yet by asking me to leave her house. That wasn't on my terms or playing into my need to declare that I was the one running away. I was absolutely licked, and I knew it deep inside of me. I was thin as a rail sitting on that couch, because I never ate when I was on meth, and I had been flying from high to high. I couldn't seem to go a day without some kind of substance in my body. The beast could go on devouring me like that, or I could try to fight him off, but that required hope. Was I worth hoping for? I really couldn't believe such a thing on that day. The most I was capable of was telling my mom I would go talk to the counselor because I realized my life was trashed.

STOPPING
THE BEAST
IN ITS TRACKS

CHAPTER 10

I LIKE TO CALL the day I stopped my beast in his tracks my first glimpse of hope. I didn't know I could begin to believe in myself just by seeing a crowd of sober kids hanging out laughing, talking, and running around having the time of their lives. It gave me the realization I didn't have to choose our family legacy of addiction to see the kids at the twelve-step center where my mom took me after I agreed to talk to a counselor. It wasn't the fact that all of them seemed genuinely happy that got to me. It was the fact that they all seemed this way without a single drug in their body. How could that be? It was possible, though; that's the only thing I knew for sure.

I didn't immediately decide to change the day my mother forced me to choose between leaving the house and entering a new recovery program. I took a whole day to ponder which decision I should make. I just couldn't come to terms with another one of my mom's solutions for fixing me. To my knowledge I was unfixable, so at the beginning, my mind was completely made up and I was going to leave. I figured that there was at least one benefit to leaving. I was always welcome to stay at Steve's house, and sitting around all day getting wasted didn't seem like such a bad option for a drug addict. I called my friend Paige to ask her what she thought I should do. She told me that I was stupid and ridiculous to think I should leave and that I just needed to stop getting high and get my life together. She told me to shut up and go to the stupid program and deal with it.

I still wasn't sure what I would do after talking to Paige, and I hadn't left my room to tell my mom my decision, but then I heard her getting ready to leave the house. "I'm going with you!" The words just flew out of my mouth. She had to get Ryan, who had attended his first twelve-step meeting that night, so I jumped in the car with her. I hadn't decided to change when I got in the car, but I had decided I could at least fake it one more time and maybe, just maybe, I could get my mom off my back long enough to figure out a better plan. It was only after we pulled up at the twelve-step center that I even considered the fact that I was not in danger of becoming some parent-obeying, straitlaced, rule-abiding teen if I decided to change. I hopped out of the car in the parking lot and fell in with Ryan's friends. They weren't lame.

It seemed like these kids had taken their lives back. I remembered when I used to own my life and knew I wanted to get back to that place, but letting myself think about things like that gave me a sense of fear that hurt so much. As I stood in the parking lot, my head began spinning with a hundred questions. Did I want to enter into another rehab? Was it going to be a waste of time? Was I just a waste of time? I was consumed by so much dread. What would life be like if I were sober? Would I hate every minute of it? Would it be like waking up from a nightmare only to realize I also hated my life when I was sober? While using I felt like I could conquer the world, yet I was too high to follow through with any of my dreams. I craved excitement and a daring lifestyle. What if a lifestyle like that was impossible for a sober person?

If I left home I did know I could expect to be daring. Besides going to Steve's place, I was sure I would end up all right on my own and be able to support myself by becoming a stripper. I wouldn't need anyone then to take care of me or get me high because I would be able to live without anyone telling me what to do or who I should be. This dark and untrusting side of me spoke up loudly against the hope I felt. In my sick head I was trying to talk myself out of believing I was worth a try. I told myself there was no way in the world that all these kids could be as happy as I thought they seemed and not be high on something. It just wasn't possible, or maybe they were just more normal than I had become over the years and were happy because they had been the kind of kids that broke curfew or ditched school functions and drank here and there, but not the kind of kids that had been to the depths that my addiction had taken me. The hopeful side of me said I was wrong to believe any of that.

At this point all I knew was that nothing had worked for me so far, and getting high wasn't really working for me either. I had tried to stop with my own will, and that didn't work. I was hospitalized, and that didn't work. I threw myself into church, and that also didn't work. All I knew is that whatever it was that was going to save me had not been introduced into my life just yet. Why not this? The new hope inside me said that the kids I met at the twelve-step group were just like me. They were just further along, and to get there what I needed to do was make a decision to try again.

I told my mom I wanted to join the kids I had met in the parking lot the night we picked Ryan up. I met with a counselor after that and was set up to begin recovery. I was absolutely terrified walking into my first newcomer meeting. My mouth was dry, my heart raced, and a huge hole inside of me throbbed for some kind of fix. I quickly noticed just how attractive the counselor who was running the meeting was. He looked like a model with long hair pulled back in a ponytail. Each time he spoke to me, I ate up the attention and felt at ease. After the introductions in our group, he began to tell parts of his story, and it was as if he was telling my story, which completely captured my attention. He began to describe desperation and a loneliness that I identified with so much. Up to this point, no one had ever come even close to understanding the kind of hell that my addiction had taken me to. No one had ever gotten past the wall of anger I had built around me. Since this counselor broke through to me so quickly, I knew that something was available for me at that place if I would just stay and keep listening.

Something said to me at that meeting has stuck with me to

this day. As the counselor told his story, he shared with me that he decided to stop using because he just "became sick and tired of being sick and tired." This felt like it came from God's mouth, and I was completely blown away. I had never had the experience of a simple phrase reaching to the deepest parts of my soul. It reached even to the part of me that wanted to fight the choice I had made to try again to stop using drugs, and it filled up the part of me that wanted to live. Nothing at my meeting went the way I had planned. I expected to show up and be told that I was a really screwed-up kid, that I was breaking my parent's heart, that drugs were the devil, and that I was going to end up in a gutter someday unless I got sober. That wasn't the case, and that made this rehab different from every other counselor, doctor, hospital program, or consequence I had had forced upon me. I knew for a long time, with 100 percent of my mind, body, and soul, that I had a problem with alcohol and drugs. No one had ever put that problem to me the way the counselor did at my first newcomers meeting. He said that I had the potential to have a condition called alcoholism.

This counselor had given my beast a name. I was told that the illness of alcoholism is an addiction that transpires through family generations without regard for race, age, faith, gender, intelligence, profession, or even the general nature of a person. I became a little more comfortable really considering that I might have an illness, not just a habit. The illness of addiction is a family affair, which is why it is a nightmare everyone in my family had visit them at one point or another, and why it was a beast in our lives that each of us had to face. Addiction gets passed on even if you didn't ask for it, or you can't handle it, or you don't know it is about to consume you. Information like this actually got through to me, but that didn't mean I was about to give the information my immediate trust. I was still wary of committing to anything. I hadn't decided to stop using; I had only decided I should try again because what I had heard about my behaviors was new.

During my newcomers meeting, I was asked to commit to staying sober and attending the meetings for thirty days. I couldn't even handle going one day without using. I wondered how I was going to go thirty days, because that seemed like an eternity to me. I also believed at this point that I was still capable of using and fooling everyone around me that I wasn't. This kind of thinking seems funny to me now. It's usually pretty obvious to everyone else when an addict continues to use. My counselor proposed a deal, though. He told me that if I gave him thirty days, he would get my mom off my back, so I agreed to go along with his deal. If nothing else, I was going to at least pretend I was clean. At this time I was heavily involved in huffing, a way to use any kind of chemical vapor to get high. It wasn't likely I was going to be able to keep my promise to the counselor in that position. I huffed during my thirty days because it was just so easy to do. I could go into anyone's bathroom and get high off a can of air freshener spray. I felt out of control if I didn't huff or use the old drugs or alcohol I was used to. Getting high was what felt normal to me, and being sober was the feeling that was weird to handle.

There was also the same old friendship dilemma at recovery that I had had all my life. I hadn't really gotten to know anyone well in the group, and in that new place of being vulnerable, I didn't have a desire to. I felt so out of place at the sober functions. I put on a happy face as a huffer and pretended for everyone there that I was sober, but on my own time I was back with the friends I wasn't ready to leave. I had status in these groups with people that were older, popular, and had money. On the weekends I was still going to hardcore parties, where I would come across many people that I had known from church that I never thought would have touched a drug in their life. These were the altar boys and girls and the kids that were youth leaders. I quickly learned that they were just as into the drug scene as I was, and some were in even worse. A few were huffers that were actually pretty out of control considering just how dangerous it can be. Huffing can kill the very first time.

Everything outside of my meetings at recovery completely revolved around my using. I received constant phone calls from people who needed drugs and people who wanted to give me drugs, and I was consuming more drugs than I ever knew anyone could. With the amounts that I was huffing, it is a miracle that I didn't find myself dead. Inside of rehab I tried to duplicate the fastest way I had learned to make new friends and not feel alone. I looked for the kids who were still getting high. We would sneak off after the meetings while everyone was hanging out at the coffee shop, where I had seen the kids who were so happy on the night I had that glim-mer of hope. I didn't really understand at the time that most kids in recovery were there because they actually wanted to be sober. What I had seen was real. I just wasn't ready to do the work yet to make that hope true for me. It had to go in small phases for me, so when

I believed in myself enough to try again, this was a huge accomplishment. It just didn't change my thinking right away. I couldn't comprehend why anyone would want to be sober after I had temporarily been forced to experience it in contrast to the euphoria given by drugs and alcohol.

Eventually it was clear to the counselors that I was involved in the downward spiral of many of the kids in the program. I would go use with kids and then sneak back and act like we had been at the coffee shop the whole time; all the while we were so paranoid that everyone would know. When the counselors confronted me, it was because someone had ratted me out. The confrontation was the last thing I wanted to happen again to me at that time, after what I went through with Lindsey. I found out I would have to go through that all again when I was approached before the start of a meeting by one of the kids who regularly got high with me. I could tell right away just how upset and irate he was. He accused me of telling the counselors that I had got him high and proceeded to tell me that someone had given a list of names of all the kids in the program who were still using. I tried to convince him that it wasn't me who told. My loyalty was to drugs, not the program, I explained.

The list of names piled up after that. Some of the kids on the list ended up leaving recovery, and those that were in positions of leadership were forced to step down. I figured the outcome for me was going to be another boot out of a rehab program, but as the days went by, I didn't get kicked out. The lack of scare tactics set this recovery program apart and so did the bright idea to draw a person like me in closer at the starting stage of getting clean. I was put into inpatient to be counseled more closely after it was discovered I was still using, which was the opposite action of every other program I had been in. I didn't know I was being switched to inpatient. I fumed, on the defensive, at the meeting where I found out, instantly throwing up all my walls. I was certain that people didn't have a clue what kind of girl they were messing with. I was ready to play hardball to keep things the same as they had been in every other program, where I was the one who was in control.

My mom was supposed to be leaving that weekend for a camping trip with her boyfriend, Bob, and his kids, but she told me we just had to stop by the twelve-step center before she left to talk about Ryan's homecoming. What I didn't know was that he had told my mom I was using and that he couldn't return home because of my addictions. I was so angry when I realized that I had been lied to about the purpose of the meeting. It wasn't about Ryan at all. So there I was, sitting on the floor in the coffee shop at the twelve-step center, feeling very alone and very uncertain of my future. I had been going to the rehab functions, I had been attending the meetings, and I had even drunk the damn coffee like I was supposed to. A counselor stayed with me the whole time I vented and raged. She was cool, letting me smoke all her cigarettes. Little did I know that it was just one of her tools to get me to trust her and open up, so the program was in control, not me. At this time I had no idea that my mother had already left the meeting and was checking out the residential house that counselors wanted me to attend.

It seemed like forever that I sat and talked to the counselor. She told me her rehab story, about how she came to sobriety and all the trouble she had gotten herself into before. This caused me to open up and give her some of my history as a user. What I said probably only helped confirm how badly I needed inpatient treatment, and that it needed to happen very soon. The talk wasn't enough to keep me from wondering what was taking my mother so long in the meeting, because I still didn't know the meeting about my brother was never the plan in the first place. I began to ask for her. Next thing I knew I was sitting in an office surrounded by counselors, being told the truth. I should have known that I was walking right into my own intervention. I could feel the fear coming over me that I felt in the parking lot the night I first visited the twelve-step center and could hear my heart beating in my ears. The most frightening part of an intervention for an addict is to hear that a different life is possible, and that this life is actually better. It is an unbelievable concept that brings up all the what-if questions I had already asked myself.

Yet I had seen the evidence. There was a way for me to be happy, free, and sober. I knew my life was still the opposite. I wasn't dumb. I knew how badly off I was and I definitely didn't need that pointed out to me over and over again. I had lived my life thinking and knowing in my heart that I probably wasn't going to see my eighteenth birthday. This had been a reality I came to live with at some point years before, when I shut off all of my emotions from even caring that death was probably going to be my destiny. I just accepted that as a fact of what happens to a person who takes the amount of mind-changing chemicals I did. *No way, no way, no way,* I repeated in my head as the counselors explained the plan to move me to the residential home run by the twelve-step center. The suggestion of inpatient treatment brought me right back to the scary hospitals I had seen, with the bars on the windows, the freaky kids that drooled, and Santa Claus, who declared I was beyond help. I only began to listen when the counselors mentioned the fact that the program took place at a house, not an institution.

The program seemed like a regular day at home. There was not a bedtime rule, and I could stay up to hang out all night if I wanted to. I wouldn't be subjected to terrible hospital meals and could cook anything I wished to in a community kitchen. It was going to be like a forty-five-day vacation to pick myself back up again. That explanation didn't sound so bad. The counselors just needed an answer. That's when the what-if questions filled me to the top. The biggest question was whether I was done using, because I wasn't sure I really was. I had a huge drug party planned. I also had two days left of school I needed to make up if I was going to get any credit for that year. I brought up the reality of my school situation as a way to say no to treatment at first, but the counselors rejected this. They assured me that they would let the school know my situation and were positive that the school would waive the two make-up days. "You have given your getting-high career 100 percent," a counselor finally said. "What would happen if you gave this 100 percent?" This question got to me. She was right. It was that one moment of clarity that I desperately needed to hear.

My mind was caught up at the same time with thoughts about the drug party. Nothing could shake that as my secure place that I wanted to get to no matter what. I never got there. I was given two options by the counselors: go to residential treatment now, or choose to go camping with my mom and Bob. I chose to go camping and let this whole thing sink in. I had agreed to enter the residential house on the condition I could finish up my last days of school, where I knew I could at least party with my friends before disappearing. I partied all night at Robert's house after I finished my classes. We were back to speaking because I'd go back to him when I needed drugs, but then I got to a place where I had no way to tell him what was about to happen for me. I was about to be gone for six weeks at the residential house, so I told him that I would be on vacation and would call him when I got back. He drilled me, like always. Where was I going? Why? There was no way that I could tell him I was going to treatment because I knew if I had let him, Robert could have talked me out of it. My glimmer of hope led me in good directions when it was encouraged by people that wanted me to get well. Robert wasn't one of those people. I woke up from partying with him with a horrible hangover and just tried to keep myself busy, packing for inpatient, so I didn't have to completely freak out and shut down.

It felt kind of good when the counselor actually came to my house to take me to treatment. That personal connection made the counselors at the twelve-step center different from other counselors I'd known. I felt very much taken care of, and it calmed my nerves some. I was taken to a group session when I arrived at the residential house and met the two other housemates who were admitted to the house. The house held ten beds that were given to five girls and five boys. Over the next few days a roommate joined me, and that helped to make me feel more comfortable. She seemed so much like me. We were both regular girls that just liked to get high too much. We went to group with everyone else in the house, and it was a very intense experience. We covered everything from our stories of using to our beliefs about God to learning about honesty to connecting to our fears. There was no rock left unturned. The group would often focus on one of us at a time while the others listened and gave input. I was given a nickname I loved, "Fireball." I was becoming the spunky, outspoken, fiery redhead I remembered I was around these people. The name made me proud! Everyone knew who they were talking about when the name was mentioned.

I had a hard time being totally honest, even with these people that clearly cared for me. We were asked how much sobriety each of us had, to give ourselves the best chance possible to achieve total sobriety. I, of course, stuck to my story of several weeks sober that I usually told when anyone would ask. I would just make a number up off the top of my head. My group saw straight through my lie and called me on it. One session became focused on trying to get me to be honest about my real length of sobriety. All I knew about being confronted at that time was that it felt threatening, which made me feel like I couldn't back down. I felt like I would lose all the credibility that I had just barely started to build in my life if I didn't go head to head with the counselor. I thought what would happen if I became honest was that the people in my group would never ever be able to trust me again.

There is so much shame attached to addiction. When I wouldn't get honest with my group, it was just my disease trying to deceive me again into thinking that I didn't have a disease. I was a long way from believing I could ever be accepted for what I was. My coping skills told me to put up my walls, give them attitude, run, and try to get high. So that is exactly what I did. I waited until the evening meeting. When I saw there were other group members I could lose myself between I disappeared out a side door with my phone book in hand and didn't look back. I decided that it probably wouldn't be smart if I went to the pay phone just a few yards away on the corner, so I decided to walk down the street a little ways to a more discreet phone. I was a few hundred feet away from the phone booth when a car pulled up next to me and out jumped a couple of counselors. Again, they were drawing me in as I was trying to force them to reject me or get them to kick me out.

I was busted but surprised enough that they would come find me, and the counselors kept showing up, one after another, each one taking a turn to intervene and try to reach me. As I sat on the back tailgate of one counselor's truck, I just kept chain-smoking and clenching my phone book tightly. I wasn't willing to get honest, and I knew that I couldn't go back for the long haul unless I became willing to get honest. I would call some-one as soon as the counselors left and I'd get away. Next thing I knew, up drove a black Mercedes Benz. The passenger door flew open and out stepped the founder of the program, which stunned me. His words were pretty harsh. He obviously wasn't happy that I had taken off, and he threw it in my face that I was tossing away what might be my last chance to get this right. He asked me if I would go back and give it at least twenty-four more hours.

This I agreed to do. I surrendered my phone book filled with drug connections and the numbers of my party friends.

The next day group was the same old story. It was a full-court press to get me honest. I was confronted about my length of sobriety and was still too scared and nervous to actually tell the truth or admit I had lied, so I kept to my original story. After a couple of hours of being grilled and probed I became furious, just like I had before, and decided I had had enough and was going to leave. The counselor pointed toward the door and told me that I was free to go. My head spun. *What?* This question turned to *whatever.* As I walked out the door, I could feel all eyes on the back of my head, and as I stepped outside, I was faced with the fact that I was alone. I had turned my back on people trying to help me, but I had just wanted to get out of there, and that's when I realized I had signed up to figure out my next move in life on my own. Right off, I was going to call Steve. The problem was, I had only a few of my belongings and was absolutely broke. It was like being stuck out with Christy with our tin of coins. I ended up resorting to nickels and dimes again. I asked the first guy I came across if he had a quarter that I could borrow so that I could make a phone call, hoping desperately that he wouldn't tell me no.

The guy didn't hesitate to pull the change from his pocket. He fished out two quarters and reached to hand them to me. "Why don't you take them both; you might need the extra one." *How generous,* I thought as I headed back to the pay phone. I put his first quarter in and dialed Steve's number, but before I could say hello, the phone was hung up. I turned around to see who had ended my call and was surprised to see a fellow group member, his finger holding down the receiver. I was overcome with confusion and then anger. This guy was actually trying to stop me again, making it impossible for me to get the heck out of Dodge. I screamed at him, "What do you think you're doing?" He then proceeded to tell me that I was making a big mistake and that I shouldn't leave. That just made me surer than ever that I needed to get away. Soon he realized that nothing was going to make me stick around, and he took off. I let out a sigh of relief when I realized that I still had the second quarter. By then I would have fought off anyone who even thought about hanging up my phone call.

I called Steve's house. He picked up and asked if I had just called and hung up on him. I told him I had, but that it was a very long story, and I asked him if he could come and get me. As I waited for Steve to show, I started to feel very uneasy because at any moment counselors might swarm me and try to get me to decide I wanted to go back to group. I wasn't surprised when this happened. My group counselor came walking around the corner, clearly searching for me. I had to do something quickly, before Steve arrived, that much was for sure. He didn't know I had been at the residential house, and that was the way I wanted it to stay. It was a huge embarrassment for me to be there at that time. I didn't want all my friends sitting around getting high, talking about how I ended up not being able to handle it in the end. I grew more nervous as my counselor approached me, feeling very unsure of what was going to happen, but nothing really did. The counselor looked me dead in the eyes at that point. "I love you and I hope you don't die," she said. The counselor hugged me and turned around, and then she walked off and didn't look back.

I can remember so vividly that when Steve finally pulled up after that, I was in complete disbelief. He arrived in his aunt's car and was wearing these sunglasses that had a picture of a marijuana leaf on the front corner of them. This at least confirmed for me that I had made the right decision about whom to call. All I wanted to do was get high anyway. I jumped in the car without hesitation, and we headed off to his house to party. Steve got me high, and we spent the rest of that afternoon smoking joint after joint. The whole time I heard my counselor's voice in my head saying, "I love you and I hope you don't die." The sound of her voice and the words began to kill my high, and the higher I got to try to forget, the more depressed I became, and the more I wanted to die. After hours of sitting there it started to sink in that this death wish was all I had. Unless I did something to change it, this would be my life, day in and day out. All my life would be doing nothing and then getting high, getting high and then doing nothing. I finally spilled my guts to Steve and told him the whole truth about where I had disap-peared to. Then I got up off the floor and told him, "I know I have to go back."

The bottom line was that I didn't set out to have a crappy life—no one does—but I was born into a legacy of family addiction that I didn't know I could choose to change. I had walked away from the best thing that probably had ever happened to me. When I realized that I had, I chose to walk myself back.

THE TRANSFORMATION

CHAPTER 11

I HAD STEVE take me to my mother's house after I chose to go back to the residential house. I had a few hours before the next group meeting and used the time to explain to my mother and Bob that I had run away from group but that I truly had a desire to try again. While I was waiting for my meeting to roll around, there was a huge battle in my head. My addiction was still fighting for its life, while the rest of me, which had decided to hope, was ready to experience the feelings of my real life. When I arrived at the coffee shop, my counselor asked me to explain to my fellow housemates why I had left and why I wanted to come back. At this point I knew that if I stood any chance of them allowing me back,

I would have to get honest about my real length of sobriety. To their knowledge I had ten days sober, which was the truth at that time, but that was before I had run away with Steve and got high. This was my last chance, so I told them that I had ten days sober even though that was a lie, because it was as close to honest as I was capable of being.

I was paranoid that I might not be let back in if the group knew I had relapsed that very same day. After I pleaded my case I was asked to step out of the room. It was up to the group whether I was going to be allowed to return. I paced back and forth, fully feeling like the decision they were making was a life or death one for me. When they called me back in, I was greeted with hugs from every group member and counselor, welcoming me back. I hadn't come completely clean with them, but it was the closest to the truth that I had come in a very long time. I spent the next weeks in group, listening, talking, and arguing. I began to go through a process to change my old ways of thinking and to evaluate my decision-making skills as they had functioned in the past so I could learn new tools to help me make better decisions to stay sober in the future. This process included taking a closer look at the people that had been in my life. I came to the conclusion that they were all there for the same reason: so I could use them either for drugs or for getting loaded. This included everyone from my best friends to acquaintances to even my own boyfriend, when I had dated Robert. I realized that there was no one in my life, no one that I had surrounded myself with, that I could count on to understand the place I had reached.

At the very bottom, transformation only happens at the moment the pain becomes extreme. Nobody I knew at that time could have understood I was at the end of my using, whether that meant getting sober or pushing myself to die an addict. I was choosing to use the pain I felt at the bottom to work my way back up to a normal life. I could have transformed myself in death just as easily by choosing to let the bottom drop out when I hit it and then free-fall until my life ended. But to live and do the opposite now meant I had to completely surround myself with new people who didn't get high, didn't drink, and were sober. Because I didn't have the tools yet or the willpower to say no, it was crucial that I cut ties with everyone who could or would enable me to use. During inpatient treatment I wrote a number of letters cutting ties with people that I knew I couldn't have in my life. One of the hardest letters for me to write was to Robert. As far as he knew I was still on vacation.

The letter I wrote Robert was very short and blunt and gave no details of my whereabouts. I had a good idea that it would not be the last contact that I would have with him if I were to tell him where I was, knowing that he would want more answers than those that I gave him in the letter. Also while in inpatient I received a letter from my father. It was postmarked from the Yavapai County jail, where he had been locked up following a third conviction for driving under the influence. I knew everything the letter was going to say before I even opened it. By then I distrusted his promises. I guess you could say that I was not surprised or even excited to read all the empty vows to me that things were really going to be different this time. The letter read:

Dear Lauren & Ryan,

How are you kids doing? I wrote you a couple of weeks ago but I haven't heard from you. I was hoping you'd write. I'd like to hear from you. I miss you very much. I hope you're not mad at me for anything. I know I haven't done right by you in the past but I've changed. I've been in classes and counseling for seven weeks now and I'm feeling good about my progress. I've come to an understanding that I can't drink ever again. I'm working on my attitude and trying to deal with feelings and emotions that I've hid from you and others and most of all myself. It's very hard to realize one's faults and problems. To admit I have a problem and take action to fix the problem is one of the hardest things I've ever done. But I will make it and get through it a better man and father for it.

I want to be your dad again. To spend good times together. I want to be able to help you with your problems and you can help me with mine. I hope that when I get out in August and I get settled that you can come and visit me. I'd like to set up some kind of regular schedule for phone calls and visits with you. We need to spend more time together. We need to get to know each other again. I don't want us to get any further apart. We're family and we need to be close. I need to be close to you. I'm not the same man or dad you knew. I think you'll like me.

Well kids I have to go. I've got a counseling session that I need and don't want to miss. So please write me and tell me how you are and what you're doing. I love you both very much. And I'll make you proud of me.

Love, Dad

This was just one more thing for me to bring up in group so I could get support for my emotions instead of getting high to make them disappear. I was learning to make new decisions about who to keep in my world. Was I going to start any type of relationship with my father once he was out of prison? Part of me didn't want to believe him that anything would ever change, because I didn't know if I could handle being hurt by him once again. This led me to realize why my addiction was such a powerful illness. I had been using it to numb my feelings, so I didn't have to feel the pain. This was nothing new for a person in my family. I was so much like my father was at that time and what my mother used to be. It was through her family that she learned that addictions held this power. It was realistic to ask if I would be able to stay sober even if my father didn't, and that brought me pain. With the help of my counselors, I was able to sit down and write my father a letter about these thoughts. I let him know that I was also trying out sobriety and that it was important for me to surround myself with sober people. I told him I would love for him to be in my life if he was able to stay sober. At the end of the letter I wished him luck and told him that I loved and missed him so much.

Once I wrote the letter, part of me became very excited. I

thought that maybe this was a new beginning, not just for me, but for my whole family. At this point I needed optimism as a way to look forward to and be excited about life. It opened new doors in my imagination. I tried to fathom what it would be like if my father were sober. My whole life, I barely ever saw him this way. I came to the realization that I couldn't imagine my father sober because I had no clue what type of person my father was without his alcohol, and he had no clue what type of person I was without my addictions. If we did reconnect, we were going to have to get to know each other all over again.

In group therapy I was making progress but continued challenging some of the concepts the counselors were trying to teach me. In day-to-day life, the choices they recommended seemed so difficult to make. They told me that I had to change three things in my life: people, places, and things. To imagine changing all this was the same as giving up everything I knew. I fought against changing so much all at once. I had let Robert know that I didn't want to see him, but my head told me that I could handle being around my other friends that used because I just wouldn't go back to using. I felt loyalty to these friends, and I couldn't grasp the concept of turning my back on people that I had known for years just because some counselor I had known for two weeks told me to. Over time it became obvious I was wrong. The one thing that I had never tried before in my life was to change my circle of friends. Even during the time I had been involved in the youth group at my church, when I tried promises to God and to myself that I would change, I refused to hang out with anyone who didn't get high.

I always had a sixth sense for seeking out the people who were addicts. I went on church retreats and had plenty of opportunities to make friends that were clean, or to stop using, but it never worked because I found users that kept me focused on my addictions. While on the retreats I would roll joints on the bus with other users, and we would spend our time in the woods getting high. The retreats gave me plenty of time to think about the way my life was going, which at the time seemed like it was going fine. It thrilled my mom that I was willing to try the retreats. She thought that maybe these would save me. The retreats did help me to realize that I was heading down the wrong path. I wanted something more in my life than the empty and hollow feeling I had inside. When I came home and told my mom I had decided to give up drugs, I did think I could do it. Once I got back to my regular routine, I couldn't. I went right back to hanging out with my old friends and lost any of that hope for a better way. That kind of cycle became a repetitive one until I got that first glimmer of hope at the parking lot of the twelve-step center. The kids I saw there were sober because they had surrounded themselves with sober people. That was the change I hadn't tried.

I was easily influenced all my life. I would do anything to feel part of a group or get an opportunity to lead. It connected with me when my counselors kept telling me that if I was going to continue to hang around with people who got loaded, then I was most likely going to end up loaded, too. To me being accepted by people was just like getting high, except on an emotional level, so my counselors were right. I was willing to go to any lengths to gain acceptance, whether that meant doing drugs or stealing money or telling lies. I felt good when I was accepted by a group of people and bad when I was not. All of it was to try to fill this void inside of me that was caused by an absent father. My effort to feel whole became its own addiction, and so I was scared to let go of the nonsober people I depended on to make me feel okay. I was also okay when I could go to safe places where I knew I would be welcomed, but my counselors said I had to stop.

One of my favorite places to go to was a pool hall, where I spent countless nights drunk with friends trying to shoot pool. Bars had been out of the question because I was too young to get in, so the pool hall was the one place that was open late that we could smoke in. I can't recall a time that I ever made it to the pool hall sober or left without a high. In my reality, everyplace I went was related to my using, and this included the pool hall, church, and school. I hooked up in those places with people who could get me high. I went to school only to score dope. My friends would leave me lines on the toilet lid, and we would take turns going to the restroom to get high. I had friends who would bring me chaser beers for my hangover cure in the mornings, and I would plan my day according to who had the dope and what house I could go to smoke out and spend the rest of my day. I had even memorized the bus schedules to my dealer's house.

Living at the residential house pushed me to learn about feelings I had not allowed myself to experience. I was an angry, guilty, unfulfilled, drug-abusing, alcoholic teen. I had thought that there was no other avenue left for me to take by a certain point and that no possibility existed for happiness or a good quality of life without drugs and alcohol. I had no idea how to cope with all the new feelings that were coming out when I admitted these things. After I stopped self-medicating with my addictions, feeling real pain transformed me. My spirit was broken, I realized, in addition to the physical and emotional parts of me. At the residential house, all of these dimensions came into focus through the twelve steps, which was a different system from other approaches I had tried. When I would throw myself into church, leaders there dealt only with the soul. At the hospital or in rehab it was mostly about getting physically clean. When I put my faith in the power of personal transformation that the twelve-step program teaches is possible, I experienced honesty about all three dimensions.

In group counseling, I got honest about my need for acceptance. I understood that I would resist making changes to my friends and to the places that I went because I had built up a life that put me in the center of all these things, where I had always wanted to be. My counselors respected my need for acceptance and recognition and fed that need in a positive way. That's why I had been drawn in closer to them each time I tried to quit the program or run away. I was being given a lot of attention and positive feedback because the way to stop me from using drugs was to give me something better than the drugs. Treating people positively was designed into the program. It gradually changed my definition of happiness. For example, seeing all those kids having a great time without drugs and alcohol was unbelievable. It brought me to the realization that before, I didn't have a clue how to even choose friends that encouraged me to be happy. I had to be taught a lot of things over again about living a normal life, so I threw myself into the recommendations of the program.

Every day of the week I went to meetings, hung out at the coffee shop at the twelve-step center, and went to sober dances and functions. I got to know people but also let them get to know me. It was a time of self-discovery because along with allowing others to get to know me, I was also getting to know myself. It became apparent to me that I didn't have a clue about my likes or dislikes. Choosing to write letters to cut ties or to think about the places I needed to stop hanging out caused me to consider who or what I might like to fill those spaces in my life. For so long the drugs were the only thing in my life that decided whether I liked or disliked something. Addiction totally consumed me to the point that I walked around in a fog for years; therefore, I never had the time for growth and discovery. I wasn't able to tell you my favorite color, my favorite activities, or even the type of movies I enjoyed the most.

There came a time to put all of the tools that I learned in the residential house to use. To help me understand how, I got a sponsor. A sponsor is a mentor for people who are trying out sobriety, and the sponsor is able to counsel about problems that always come up in everyday life during recovery. Sponsors have previously worked through the steps themselves. Eventually I was going to head back home, and my sponsor was the one who would be there to help me work through the twelve steps. It was an accountability system that I had never tried before when I started this next phase. An addict's thinking is broken by the time recovery begins, I learned, so even addicts with many years of recovery still can't rely on their own thinking to run their lives. Sponsors even have sponsors. Everything the sponsor says is a suggestion, but the suggestions help to get thinking and decision making redirected toward a more positive direction. I once heard someone with thirty years of sobriety say, "I know I can help you and you can help me, but because my thinking is broken, I know I can't help myself."

With my sponsor on board, after six weeks at the residential house I was discharged to the recovery's outpatient program. It was four hours a day for another six weeks. Thank goodness for the continued contact with the people I knew from the residential house, because it helped make the transition feel safe, and along with my sponsor, the shift gave me a support system for returning to my home life outside of the constant watch of counselors. I had a new circle of friends that were all sober and that wanted to see me succeed.

The house was now a totally sober environment to return to. My mom had experienced her own personal power to keep changing. She gave up the glasses of wine she had been drinking before that time. It just seemed that life was waiting for us, though. Immediately my past came tearing at me, and I had to deal with life on life's terms. It didn't take long for Robert to find us, and by then he was very angry about where I was spending my time. He showed up at the twelve-step center looking for me. I had no clue he had even surfaced. My mom came home one night and told me she needed to talk to me about something. I instantly knew something was wrong.

I was actually kind of scared when she told me that Robert

had found out where I was and where I was receiving treatment. But my nervousness instantly turned to anger when I realized that everyone but me had known what was going on and had kept the news from me. I approached my outpatient counselor about the fact and was furious. I demanded to know why he didn't tell me what was going on the whole time. "Why didn't anyone tell me that he had shown up?" Standing in the middle of the coffee shop, the counselor looked at me with the most honest face that I had ever seen and said, "You are safe here." What he meant was that these people had my back. The fear and nervousness that had been pumping through my veins instantly subsided, and I was overcome by a sense of calm and trust. It was then that I knew what he had been talking about when he said that the love of the group is a power greater than myself and could do me no wrong.

I was beginning to learn how to trust something other than drugs for the first time in my life. This felt so good. Not long after my family had a protective order served against Robert, he showed up at our house, banging on the windows, trying to get me to come out. I hid while my mom called the police. I knew in my gut that this would not be good. He was an angry person as it was, and I had lied to him about where I had been when I lived at the residential house. Then I had sent him a letter by mail telling him I never wanted to see him again. It was a recipe for disaster. I knew that my leaving him in this fashion was probably going to enrage him when I mailed his letter, but I was not willing to be controlled by him anymore. I knew that if I went out and talked when he showed up at my house and banged on the window, it would have been a backward step that probably wouldn't have ended peacefully. I let the cops handle it instead. By the time they got there, Robert was already gone. A search of the neighborhood turned up nothing.

He didn't give up and then filed suit to get the order of protection that my mom had filed against him taken off. I was petrified when I found out this suit meant I would have to testify against Robert in court to make the order stick. I thought there was no way that I could face him. I had been working so hard in outpatient to learn a better way of life, and I felt like all of this was holding me back and was just making it that much harder to believe in my glimmer of hope. I imagined that most addicts got to disappear after deciding to get sober and got to recover away from everything and everybody else. If that was true, it sure wasn't true for me. I couldn't escape my old life, it seemed like, no matter what I did. I felt a little better knowing that a counselor from my twelve-step program was going to be with me in court. It gave me a sense of security and trust that I had done the right things. I also knew that going to court was the only way I was truly going to walk away from this part of my life, and Robert, forever. Things always had to go to the extreme for me before they could change, so I went to court to testify, and with my counselor and my mother by my side, we won. The judge upheld the ruling. With that behind me, I was able to get back to dealing with my recovery and myself. I really felt like I could never turn back after that point.

I had been given a chance by dealing with Robert to really put to use all the tools that I had learned. The knowledge was there before that, and the support was there. The experience had just been the first time it was up to me to apply the tools where and when I needed to. I never could have figured that out before, how to deal with a situation like Robert on my own and still stay sober. I would have hurried to a high that turned the emotions all off. I wasn't going to choose to live that way anymore. I was told that as I worked at my recovery, I was going to feel pain as a sober person and that the pain was going to hurt like hell. But nothing was painful enough in that transformation that made it worth taking a drink or using. Absolutely nothing was as good as the feeling that came after the pain, either. We never had Robert problems again.

Feelings of success are important, but I was cautious because I worried that left to my own willpower and thoughts, I could probably talk myself into using again. This was why my transformation relied so much on trust. I wouldn't be able to talk my sponsor into letting me use no matter how bad things got. I was building a trust in my sponsor and knew she had the best intentions in mind for me. I can see now that my sponsor will always have more years of sobriety, has overcome more pitfalls than me, knows how to avoid missteps, and has more confidence in who I am than I could ever have for myself. She is the one who helped me when I began to clean up the wreckage of my past. As I dug in and cleaned out the so-called "trash" in my life and my mind, I realized that underneath there was a person whom I had hidden behind drugs and walls of anger. It is as if my transformation had to begin by peeling away the layers of an onion to reach that girl, and with each new layer I was learning how to make myself a little more humble and free. Doing that brought major self-discovery and realizations with it. I had to learn that I did not have much of a coping system. I had no accountability to anything except the drugs. I pushed away anyone who really loved me, and I saw first to the fact that I was okay and that my life was filled with people who kept enabling me.

A family addiction is a legacy because it is a story that keeps repeating itself. For an addict, the legacy ends only when these repetitions are uncovered. If they are, the family story then becomes an open book, and the beast of addiction is left powerless because the story isn't feeding on itself. I needed to peel back enough layers to make myself transparent enough to know my recovery process was working, or else I was setting myself up for dishonest behavior, which would probably lead to another relapse into the only story I had known. I knew that I might not have many chances left to get my life right that day I tore off with Steve, when I had it thrown in my face that I was about to walk away from something good. To recover or to die are intense options, and they are the only options at the bottom, yet it is so hard for addicts to see the extent of their disease from down there. It was for me. I had to sit on Steve's floor thinking about dying until it hit me. That's the kind of moment in life that makes it clear that it is a better idea to trust people that believe that you have the power to change than it is to trust yourself to evaluate life at that point. I eventually became an open book by making that choice, so now somebody will be sure to catch me before I fall back into the legacy of my family's disease.

I participated in many activities to help me learn to trust others this much, become more open-minded, and help to change my way of thinking. For so long I had such terrible self-esteem. I hated myself so much that I believed if everyone else really knew me, they would hate me as much as I hated myself. That was another reason not to trust people, and it was why it was difficult for me to open my life up like a book at first. I was very wary of letting people in for fear that they would hate what they saw. To help me come to a new way of thinking about this, a counselor had me do an activity in which all the people in the room with me were able to say one asset that they saw in me. Some of the things that I heard I felt were pretty right on, and yet there were some things said about me that I had never even noticed before. This activity helped me to start rebuilding my identity and gave me the confidence that I would need to become rigorously honest. I am grateful that my counselor wrote down all the beautiful things people noticed about me that day. I still carry them with me to this day.

I had tackled the confrontation with Robert. I knew how to draw from the strength of my family, and I was making a daily choice to live as an open book. I wanted to dive into programs at the twelve-step center to help the newcomers at this point, because I was feeling better than I ever had in my entire life.

CHALLENGES ON THE SOBER PATH

CHAPTER 12

IN SOBRIETY, I learned it was important to choose the type of people I surrounded myself with, the places I would go, and how to spend my time in activities that feed the needs inside of me that my addictions had filled before. This plan made me responsible for a different set of choices at each place on the sober path, so I chose to spend my time attending meetings and helping the newcomers that walked through the door at the twelve-step center. Those of us interested in the newcomers would meet them every day to social-ize. It was important to me that everyone had fun, or someone to talk to and connect with, for the rest of the day. A commitment to transformation was the thing I had in common with people around me. It was a choice but also a need. People understood me and could tell when there was something not right with me. Spending time with people focused on recovery was a strategy I chose to set myself up to win at life, because outside of the twelve-step center my life was continuing to evolve, which set up a series of challenges for me.

Five or six months into my sobriety I was promoted to the position of group leader when I was placed on the group's twelve-step steering committee. It was a huge accomplishment for me, and it felt as if I was instantly part of the popular crowd. This was old territory as far as my need for recognition. Everyone around me wanted my advice and friendship, and I reveled in my glory, walking around with my head a little higher at that time. I felt important for once in my life, because the people who wanted to hear what I had to say didn't want to just use me for the drugs I could give them. I sponsored several people working the group at the time and gave of myself to them endlessly. I felt like I was finally making my parents proud and proving to them, and to myself, that I could accomplish things nobody thought I ever could.

While on the steering committee, I began to become really close to those people. It was our own little clique, and we all held each other accountable. In particular I became very close to John. I had started to develop feelings for him that I had not felt in a long time, if ever. Being sober, I was able to sense the emotions of a budding relationship with every fiber of my body pumping full of euphoria. Each time that I was around John, I was overwhelmed. He put butterflies in my stomach, and there was chemistry between us neither of us could deny. He was silly and charming and energetic, and he made me want to feel that way all the time. I constantly laughed when I was around him, and eventually I fell madly in love. I was completely smitten in the beginning of the relationship. Only after seeing a different side of John did I begin to worry that this part of my sober path was one of the greatest challenges.

One minute we were fine, and the next it seemed like John hated me. The chaos of it was unsettling after I had worked so hard to choose consistent things I was accountable to. I couldn't understand why he could treat me so poorly, in part because it was so obvious that I was so in love with him in return. I just kept telling myself that things would get better, but I was constantly worried about my appearance around him, and I felt like if I looked good enough, he might love me more. If I looked like I was confident, I thought that would make him respect me. Before I knew I was in the midst of a challenge, I had led myself into a cycle from my past of making an addiction out of seeking attention. This led to verbal and mental abuse, which were things that I had not experienced before in a relationship. That stuff wasn't physical abuse, so it was hard to decide I was being abused and just walk away, even as a part of me told me that John was abusing me and that I should have walked away so many times in the relationship. He made me feel crazy for wanting to be treated well, though. I was making a decision to be a first-class citizen in other areas of my life, yet when it came to John I just let him walk all over me and lost myself in the relationship.

The dysfunction in the relationship quickly became apparent to everyone around us. My counselor approached me and confronted me about the relationship and my lack of interest in the group because of it. The counselor told me it was an unhealthy imbalance. This criticism felt horrible. I wanted to continue to be a leader, but the decision that I made to stay with John was not a good example for the other group members. The decision demonstrated that I cared about my relationship more than my sobriety. The glimmer of hope I had been following felt like it was dimming at this point, and fearful questions came back into my head, just like they always did when a challenge would put me in front of a big choice between two types of lifestyles. How could I continue to help others when I didn't even want to help myself? I chose John eventually. We were both asked to step down from the steering committee. I was so ashamed and embarrassed that I didn't even want to be around my friends anymore. When I turned eighteen, I left the steering committee and then moved up to meet with the twelve-step center's older group, where I didn't know too many people.

John was three weeks younger than I was, so when I was at the older group he couldn't go. It was hard to be at the new group without him. I felt so lonely and vulnerable, and worst of all I had been stripped of my leadership role. I lost the place where I was putting my positive energy. I started skipping out on meetings and functions just so that I could see John, and before long he and I were asked to leave altogether because we were such an unhealthy example to the others. The last straw was when John and I spent the night together on the couch at another group member's home. I was asked to leave after that by a counselor from the older group. A different counselor from the younger group approached John. We were told that our relationship was unhealthy, of course, but that we were being asked to leave the group as a result of having disregarded the advice of the counselors that we break it off. They gave us a chance to get it right and come back if we did, but I felt bullied and pushed into a corner by the counselors. On one hand, they had told me early on that John and I would make a great couple and the next minute told me I had to break it off or else I was no longer welcome.

On the other hand, I can see now that counselors knew they would not be able to help me grow anymore given the choices I was making to meet a challenging time in my life by using an emotional addiction. If I continued to meet challenges like that, the poor decisions I was making would probably lead me away from being sober eventually. I felt like the pride of sobriety had crumbled all around me that night. The sober path looked dark, and my heart felt so empty. I just wanted to be with John after that, because he was what was left for me. I wanted to make him happy so much. I changed some of the choices I made about what people to keep in my life and what places I would go after that. I had turned eighteen and also moved out of my mom's house by then, and I was living in an apartment that I shared with three other girls from the twelve-step program. After being asked to leave the group, I had to find a new place to live. Only girls from the group could live at the apartment. My mother had the same rule for me, so I couldn't go home. I eventually found a place to stay with a girl who had recently left the group on her own. She had her own apartment and was attending a different twelve-step program, but the apartment was filthy when I came to share it with her and located in a horrible part of town.

This was not my first choice for a living situation, but I had nowhere left to go after I picked my relationship with John over my role as a leader at the twelve-step program. My parents wouldn't help me out of the consequences from this choice, and my friends were no longer talking to me as a choice they were making to stay sober themselves and stay surrounded by people making better decisions than I was. There was a huge following of people that left our twelve-step center right along with us when John and I left, and this is the group I began to hang around with. I tried to keep up with meetings around town at new places. Going through all of this just added to my challenge of handling stress. The mental abuse and games were getting worse with John. He would break me down until all I could do was cry and plead for him to be nice and just love me. It was as if John really resented the situation and wondered if he even wanted our relationship at all. I had no car at the time, and I relied on John to pick me up when he could. I needed him and was back to the power dynamic in which I let somebody else have the upper hand because that person gave me the things I had to have. I would hang out all night and sleep all day with nothing else to do.

I found out I was pregnant when I was living like this. I had taken a home pregnancy test and then gone to a crisis pregnancy center to confirm that I was actually pregnant. I was not ready to be a mom, of course. I couldn't even figure out my own life. John just sat on the couch and cried when I told him the news. Talk about hitting a different kind of bottom. I was sober still while facing these facts, and I had nothing to numb away the feelings that came up. My first instinct was still hope, which was a good sign, but I hoped for John and me both, and that wasn't part of what I had learned. The choice to hope is made by the individual person. I still felt like the pregnancy was finally the thing that was going to change John. He would have to be decent to me if I had a baby. Things just got worse following the news instead.

I cried constantly and became more depressed. John would tell me that he was on his way to pick me up but fail to show. I sat by the window all night sometimes waiting for him to appear only to find out he was with all of our friends and had just decided not to come get me. It was like a wrench on my heart. I would confront him, and that's when he would break down and beg for forgiveness, which was the normal emotional chaos he brought into our lives. It left me confused and helpless. I let that mental torture continue, and I continued to be the one thing that John grew to hate. He hated me so much by the time I was a few months into my pregnancy that during a fight he pushed me, and I fell and hit my stomach into the arm of an overstuffed chair. When I hit, I felt a pain inside of me that I had never felt before. The chair hit me right where the baby was. I knew something was wrong. This was not how I wanted my life to turn out. John just continued to yell at me. I grabbed my things and ran out of the place.

Once I got back home to my apartment, I tried to lie down and rest. I called a friend to pick me up and thought that after calming down I would be able to see how everything was going to be okay. My roommate didn't see it like that. She encouraged me to walk away from John when she heard what had happened, but I didn't think I had the strength to go through the pregnancy without him. I had no idea that my mom had been in the same shoes once during her life. We both accepted a man in our lives who constantly hurt us because we doubted ourselves. I was losing the self-confidence I had gained to be a powerful person. By the evening I had started bleeding, and when I called my roommate into the bathroom to see what I saw, I told her I was scared. All I knew was that the blood couldn't be good. She called the hospital for me, and they told her what to do.

We were supposed to go to the emergency room if I was running a temperature or the bleeding was abnormally heavy. I couldn't tell how much I was bleeding. Worse, we didn't have a thermometer at the house. My friend called to borrow one, and sure enough I had a fever that was rising, so she and the friend who had loaned us the thermometer helped me into the back of a car and drove me to the emergency room. They called my parents and told them about the situation. They also called John to tell him to come be with me. At the emergency room, John and my parents all showed up, along with countless other friends and family. My blood was taken, and I was given a catheter and an ultrasound to see if the baby was okay. The doctor told me he could not find a heartbeat. Once the bleeding was stopped, I was told I could go home because nothing about the baby was conclusive just then. To know what would happen I would have to come back two days later for another blood test. If the pregnancy hormone was dropping, it would indicate that I had miscarried. I was warned this was likely going to be the case.

For the next day and a half, I lay on the couch at my apartment in constant fear that if I moved wrong, I was going to start bleeding again and kill the baby. All I wanted was for John to be there with me, and to him it was just too much to ask for. He never came. I was going through one of the scariest situations of my life, and I felt a loneliness coming back that I hadn't experienced in so long. I didn't know how to get through the emotion alone, and at this point all the courage left inside me was draining away. I was physically, mentally, and spiritually sick once again, even though I was on the sober path. John did decide to come and get me to stay the night at his place the night before I went back to the hospital, so we could go straight to the appointment together. When he picked me up, I told him that I needed to go straight to the house because I needed to continue lying down and resting. As we were on our way, he drove past one of our normal hangouts and stopped when he saw our friends gathered there instead of taking me to the house to rest.

He pulled into the parking lot and instantly started to yell at me as he parked the car, demanding that it be okay if we stopped for just a little while. No matter what I said, he didn't care, and the arguing kept escalating until we were out of the car in front of all of our friends having a screaming match. Finally, John started to kick the back of his car and get violent, which is when I raised the white flag and surrendered. I just kept repeating, "Whatever you want, John, whatever you want, John, whatever you want." As he walked up to his friends, my girlfriends came running up to comfort me. They kept asking me why I was not in bed. They had been at the hospital and heard the directions I was to follow for rest. I told them that I was supposed to be in bed staying with John for the night, but he didn't want to go straight home. When my friends asked what the fight was about, I had to admit I didn't even know. At that point I just broke down and cried.

I was too stressed out for any more of John's drama, and I was beside myself at his behavior and lack of compassion. I couldn't understand how a person could act like that. A girlfriend asked me to come with her into the bathroom to talk, and when I went in I decided to check to see if I was bleeding. Sure enough I had started gushing blood. I became really scared and shook-up once again, and I went out to tell John that we needed to go the hospital. He looked me straight in the eyes and said, *"No."* I stood there begging him to take me to the hospital, humiliated and ashamed, as all our friends watched. My best friend jumped in and said, "Lauren, I'm taking you to the hospital. Let's go." I wouldn't go with her, though. I was convinced I had to have John to make it okay. I called my mom and Bob from a pay phone and told them John had refused to take me. Bob told me to put John on the phone. After he and Bob argued back and forth, John slammed the phone down as hard as he could and told me to get in the car. I felt such a sense of relief as we drove away. I would instantly forget about all the horrible things that John had ever done after he was there for me. My mind would dismiss all the unforgivable behavior, and I would lie to myself that everything would become normal.

On my way to the hospital with John, I told him that I couldn't take all the mental abuse and torture. I told him he was about to lose me. That was when he slammed on the brakes, which spun the car around. He pulled over and repeatedly yelled at me to get out of the car. I kept saying no, but he eventually pushed me out. After he drove around for a few minutes, he pulled back up to where he had dumped me and said to get into the car. All I knew was that I needed to get to the hospital, and I didn't want to be alone, so I did get in. John then drove to a friend's house instead of the hospital, and I repeated the fact that he needed to take me now, but he refused to take me anywhere until we talked and worked everything out.

This one challenge with John was made up of several smaller challenges that I was learning how to face during early sobriety. I needed positive places to put my energy, but the pride I was taking in my leadership to newcomers at twelve-step stopped being available for me. I needed to remain accountable to other people, but because of my choice to stick with John, I was no longer welcome at supportive places like my first apartment and my house. I needed to choose options for my free time that encouraged a consistent application of the twelve steps I had learned. The apartment where I lived was disgusting, and I had nothing to do all day but think about the mess there that was a reflection of the chaos in my life. John was the one thing that I could use to fill up all the loneliness I had created for myself, yet the longer I stayed with him, the more alone I felt. I didn't know another reason why I had made the choice to hijack my sober walk by believing that this person's attention was good for me except for the fact that I had given up on the trust I had built for myself. I felt so beaten down mentally after the attention of the group was gone.

My mind was racing so fast with emotions when he took us to his friend's house to talk. I just kept telling him that I didn't want to talk anymore. One minute he was telling me he was sorry, of course,

and the next minute he was telling me that I had ruined his life. I
always wished John could just make up his mind. The next thing I
remember I was in pain, waking up on the floor at his friend's house.
I thought that from so much shouting and so many emotions, John
and I had fallen asleep. When I woke up I had a horrible pain in my
abdominal area. I could tell something terrible was happening at
that moment because it felt like I was going to die. I shook John to
wake him up and mumbled that I needed to go to the hospital that
instant or that he should call an ambulance. He told me to go back
to sleep. I could go to the hospital in the morning for the appointment I had scheduled anyway. In the end I found out I hadn't fallen
asleep. I had passed out from blood loss. John had decided to take a
nap after seeing me fall to the ground.

The voices of Mom and Bob came to me that day. They had
actually been driving around and had found me. They came in the
room where John and I were, and my mom helped me to my feet.
Bob stood over John, yelling at him, daring him to find a reason good
enough for not having taken me to the hospital. I kept telling Bob
to stop yelling at John out of instinct to do anything I could to make
John happy enough to stick by me, though I knew he never would. I
never stopped wanting him, even though he didn't want me. Before
I left with my parents, I went into the bathroom. I pulled down my
pants and saw something lying on my blood-soaked pad. The miscarriage had happened. I panicked and asked my mom to look and tell
me if she thought it was the baby. She said that she thought it was,
and she wadded it up so that we could take it with us to the hospital
to show the doctors.

The doctors confirmed that I had miscarried and told me that they would perform an autopsy to determine what went wrong. One after another, my friends and family flooded the waiting area in the emergency room. I was shocked to learn how many people were out there waiting to hear how I was. It was difficult to see that I was worth something to other people. I had believed I was worth something for a time at the beginning of my sobriety. That was what had made me decide to try, in fact. I wasn't treated like that with John. After a while I went back to believing I wasn't worth anything. It used to be like that with my dad, but even he came down to be with me from his house in Cottonwood. He came in the room and held my hand and told me that he was there for me. It was one of the first times that I ever felt like my dad had come to protect me. He was sober and finally able to be the father that I needed him to be. It was a first for us. I was so grateful for his being there. My dad said straightaway that there would be trouble if John showed up at the hospital. Even with all my family and friends there for me, all I wanted was John. I made my dad promise that he would not do anything to him.

I was hoping so much that John would come that day and be the knight in shining armor that I needed him to be. *Why not him, too,* I thought, since my dad had shown up. The nurse brought in a phone and told me somebody had called. It was John, so I told him to come to the hospital. "Yeah, but what about your parents?" he asked. He was silent when I said the baby was dead. He may have been in shock, but eventually after I told him it was okay to come down, he said he was on his way. I waited for him while having tests performed and getting a prescription. John wasn't there when it was time to leave. His brother was there in the waiting room, and when he found out I had lost the baby, his brother cried for the loss of the niece or nephew he was never going to have. It was sickening to me that John's brother could show up and reveal this kind of concern but John could not. It wasn't a surprise to everyone else. I was the only one who believed in John by then. Why did I believe? I had been kicked out of my twelve-step program because I had prioritized John. I had been kicked out of my apartment because I had prioritized John. I had lost a baby because I couldn't stop John from prioritizing himself. He had never given me any of the same sentiment.

I felt the worst that I had ever felt, like no one could understand this kind of pain. I felt like I had let everyone down and most of all myself. I rested for the next couple of days, trying to get a hold of John the whole time. When I was finally able to get him on the phone, he told me he never wanted to see me again. I wanted to know why, but that was a request for him to give me something in return again, and of course it didn't work. I wasn't welcome to call him, John told me. After that phone call we never talked again, which is when my feelings of anger, resentment, and sadness over John became evident, because I had no way out of that low place. I already looked the part of a junkie at the very bottom. It was only a matter of time before I was going to say screw it all and get loaded to numb the pain. I had lost so much weight because I couldn't eat, and I had black circles under my eyes because I would stay up all night wondering why John refused to love me. Before I made the decision whether or not to stay sober, I decided I would call the director of the twelve-step program. I hoped I would be invited to a meeting.

If I didn't do something soon, I was going to turn my addiction to useless love back into my addiction to drugs and alcohol. I needed to be surrounded by people who were making choices that led to happy, joyous decisions that were free from the influence of destructive people like John. When I called the offices and asked for the director, I was put straight through, and it was a relief to hear that the director was not surprised to get my call. I asked if it was okay if I came to a meeting, instead of waiting to be asked. The director told me to make an appointment first, to talk about my return, but that meeting didn't happen for a week. My heart was already at the meeting, so the week was the longest wait. When the director saw me at our appointment, it was obvious I had been through hell. I hadn't used, though. I told the director so and explained all that had happened since I departed from the group and told him about losing my baby. He couldn't believe I had stayed sober. "To be honest with you," he confessed, "I am not sure that you actually did." Staying sober was the one and only thing I had going for me. It was at that moment that I realized that it didn't matter what the director's opinion of me was, or what anybody's opinion of me was. The fact was that I knew what I had been through, and that I had been responsible for my failures and also my success moving past that. Nobody could take my sobriety away from me, except me, and I hadn't.

The director eventually offered me the invitation to a meeting that I hoped he would. A celebration was actually on the schedule for people that had lived at the residential house, and my mom was planning to go, so I went to that as well. I didn't know if I would go at first. If I showed up, it was possible that no one would want to talk to me for fear that I would make them look bad because I had been previously asked to leave. This wasn't a what-if fear like I had sometimes felt in the past. This fear was caused by the challenge it would be to confront the self-image that I had created in the group. I went back and forth in my head about whether or not to go, but in the end I decided that I would. I was so nervous on the way to the celebration, and I put up all my walls before walking in just in case I felt unwelcome. "Come back," said the founder of the program into my ear. He had turned his attention to me after I arrived, but before I could even hug him I broke down sobbing, and he threw his arms around me and held me tight.

There was a different kind of strength in me after this day. I made a deal with myself that I would never bend or break my principals again for the benefit of being with a person. It felt easy to say that I wouldn't, no matter how important the person was to my life. What I didn't know at the time was how much this promise to myself would be challenged as future events continued to unfold.

MY LIFE ON LIFE'S TERMS

CHAPTER 13

ONE OF THE MOST amazing gifts of sobriety is the ability to experience your own life in all its hardships and glories. The challenges are what make life so rich, because to overcome a hardship is a success that changes the way life feels. Being with another person cannot create that evolution inside. I definitely couldn't say that when I was walking around loaded, with my head in a fog. When the man I am married to today asked me to be his wife, I remember thinking, *How did I go from thinking that I wouldn't live past eighteen to having years of sober self-confidence and being about to marry the man of my dreams?* My dad was not able to find out that life becomes this rich. He had recently been released from prison when he and his new wife, Marie, came to see me in the hospital. He was sober since his incarceration yet he continued to depend on his addiction to others.

He met Marie when he was in prison. She was his drug and alcohol counselor. Because of that conflict of interest, upon his release Marie chose to quit her job. They built a new house and got married. My dad continued to attend his twelve-step meetings while he was on probation. He had finally begun to make good choices for himself. Our sobriety dates were just within months of each other, and over the course of the next five years we worked toward our sobriety, self-discovery, accountability, and trust together. I began to visit him regularly and looked forward to our time together. He was actually quite charismatic and funny and I enjoyed spending time with him. We were finally a team. I finally felt like I was getting the chance to build the relationship with him that I'd always wished for—all because we were finally sober together. But then my dad stopped going to the meetings. One Easter holiday I called him, and as soon as he answered the phone I could tell something didn't sound right in his voice. He didn't sound like the happy-go-lucky sober father I was expecting to hear on the other end of the phone. He began to tell me that Marie had left him for another man. He was devastated, he said, sobbing. He told me he didn't want to live anymore and that he had tried to kill himself. Those words were the last thing on earth that I had ever thought I would hear my father say. I fired questions at him, one after the other, about what he had done.

This was his challenge, and yet it felt like I should save him.

Why? I tried so hard to hold it together for him because he needed me, and because it was breaking my heart that he should be the loneliest person on the planet while I was with my fiancé and our families, celebrating Easter as a group. A sense of fairness is part of my character, and I don't want anyone to suffer. That didn't mean I knew how to apply what I had learned about letting addicts deal with the consequences their addiction creates. At that moment the only thing that I knew to do was to go to my father. The rest of the day was really hard. After I arrived at my father's house, I felt an overwhelming sense of fear and sadness that I had almost lost him to suicide. As I learned more about the details, these two emotions only deepened. His house was empty because all Marie's belongings and her half of the furniture were gone. There wasn't much food. Together we made an Easter dinner for my dad to eat after making a trip to the grocery store.

Over the next six months, my father tried to kill himself six more times. Because things fell apart with Marie, his recovery fell apart. His life revolved around getting Marie back and making calls to a suicide hotline. I spent countless hours on the phone with my father, trying to talk him out of further attempts on his life, and countless hours driving back and forth from Phoenix to Cottonwood to visit him in the hospitals where I discovered him after he ignored my advice. It seemed like every couple of weeks I would get a call from a hospital telling me that my dad had once again tried to die. I constantly lived in fear that the next phone call would be the one that informed me my dad was dead. To stay strong at that time, the only thing to do was attend as many meetings as I could. I was lucky to have a safety net of friends and fellow recovering addicts who were able to give me a sense of sanity, hope, and guidance. Everyone in my support group knew what I was going through, so it felt good to have a place to come to, where I could vent, cry, and heal. Because the tragedies in life arrive unexpectedly, it is crucial for recovered addicts to keep accountable to a community, sponsor, counselors, and friends. My father went the opposite direction and isolated himself. His conditioned worsened, and I received a call from the hospital to inform me that he had been put on life support.

My first thought was to pick up Ryan. Both of us were in stable places, and in the past we used to work as partners when hard times came. Then, we did drugs, but now we knew how to face hard times with different options. It was harder to handle what we saw with these options than I expected. The nurse made a point to prepare us before she allowed us to see our dad. She said we should be ready to see a lifeless body that was supposed to be our dad, with dozens of tubes coming out of him. Tears started rolling down my face when I saw it was true. Our father was in a coma. He had slit his wrists and slit his throat and received a stomach pump after arriving at the hospital to get rid of all the pills that he had downed. As I looked at all his injuries, I felt awful for believing he might have just been trying to get attention with his suicide attempts. He might have really been serious about ending it for good. I informed my grandfather about this concern, and he instantly left Montana to be with his son.

While my father was in the hospital, I stayed at his house with my grandfather. We were the same, but my dad had changed by the time he came out of the coma. He was delirious and didn't know where he was or what had happened. We had to help him learn to walk again and even learn to eat. Returning to his house after days of that, which were just so discouraging, was made even worse by the way my father had been living before his suicide attempt. In the living room there were half a dozen stains on the floor from the vomit he had thrown up convulsing from the over-dose of pills. Then I found the makings of a noose hanging from the ceiling in his garage, which had paper covering all the win-dows. Later my father would tell me that he had first tried to hang himself before slitting his wrists and throat and then consuming a couple bottles of pills.

Through all of this, I was heartbroken most because of his relapse. I was forced to think about the legacy of our family addic-tion. Why had I been able to stop repeating that story at the same time my dad was being drawn back in again and again? Obviously he was back to drinking because that was the way he knew how to cope with losing the women he was addicted to. The alcohol was his only support after they left. Without choosing to try again each time he stopped going to meetings, my dad never found a sponsor or a community of people that believed he could hope for himself. The hope is where the personal power is. I finalized my thoughts about the legacy of addiction when I opened up his fridge and saw nothing but beer. There was his support group. I knew the only option for me was to dump every bottle out. I didn't even blink because that beer was calling my name the same way it must have talked to my dad. With all that stress, I was at one of my weakest points after getting sober. The chance of getting drunk could not be an option for me. Every single time my father had the option to hope he could make a different choice, he had said pass me a bottle instead.

His last stay in the hospital really scared him, but I knew I couldn't be sure how long the scare would last, so I had my dad transferred to a Phoenix hospital near to me. While he was there he spoke to counselors, cried, talked, even attended recovery meetings. It was the first time in a long time that I felt like I could actually exhale. When I went to visit he had a little more light in his eyes. I just remember feeling hope on his behalf. He would tell me he wanted and needed to be sober, and that this was his chance to start fresh. These were old promises again, but at some point every addict who recovers says the same things and really means them. This is what makes it difficult to draw a line between yourself and the relationship you make with an addict. My dad was saying things that I had always wanted to be true for us.

During one of my visits, he told me that he wanted to start reading the *Big Book* again, the AA guide. He didn't have one, so I went to a recovery bookstore and bought him a copy. I liked being able to help lead him. I had bought him the book along with a bookmark of the Serenity Prayer, the prayer for alcoholics that was brought to the attention of an AA cofounder, who liked it so much it became a key part of the AA movement. I placed the bookmark neatly inside the pages of the *Big Book* and opened up the front cover to write my dad a note:

Dad,

Never let this book get dusty. It will save your life!
You are a miracle!

Lauren.

I felt like I was carrying hope to my father as I walked down the hall to his room. If he decided to apply everything in that book to his own life, he would make it. I'll never forget the surprised look on his face when he saw that I was back so quickly to see him. I was so proud to be able to give him a book that had been so crucial in helping me to get sober and learn to say no to our family legacy. I carried a message to another suffering alcoholic who just happened to be my dad, and after he was released from the hospital, it seemed like he was really ready to start this new life. He joined a home meeting group in Cottonwood, and this time he got a sponsor. During phone calls, my father would list the things he was doing to get involved with sober people and places. He was attending counseling a couple of times a week to help him monitor his medication for depression. This was for the pain he had to face as a result of his divorce from Marie. He also shared his hardships with me. He was frustrated at that time that his counselor had not released him back to work. He loved his work and was devastated he would not make a quick return to it.

He felt lonely and understimulated is what he said. I could tell over time that my dad was sinking deeper and deeper into a depression. He desperately wanted some kind of joy in his life, but that was something he was going to have to build up on his own. When

I realized in my own recovery that I had no idea what produced happiness for me other than my addictions, it was pretty shocking to realize I knew so little about my joy. My father didn't learn about his joy. He continued to talk about the things that were removed from him, like Marie or his work. I was constantly trying to suggest help through his counseling and medication since he was approaching recovery that way. He said neither was working anymore, which then led him back to thoughts about suicide. He called the suicide hotline so often at this point that the prevention line staff began to call me to express their deep concern.

I was trapped by the whole situation with my dad because of the role I chose to play as the hope that I wanted him to take. He wouldn't do it for himself, and I thought I could change that. I just wanted him to hold on long enough because I thought his medication might start working and then give him enough relief from his anxiety and anger that he would begin thinking more clearly. It was just a couple of weeks later when he called to say he was coming to Phoenix for a visit. I was excited to try to keep encouraging him, given the low place he had reached. I had it all planned out. It would be a great opportunity to bring my dad to my meeting, introduce him to my support group, and just get a meeting under his belt because he had given his up. When we arrived at my meeting, I cried and shared and spilled my heart out. These were the people that had given me the strength to carry through when I didn't think I could. My father got a taste of what I had been so fortunate to hear and experience. Instead of shaking my father's hand, they just pulled him in and gave him a great big hug because they had heard so much about his situation already. They told him everyone was happy he came.

As the meeting started I felt such a sense of peace. I was right where I was supposed to be, and so was my father, and both of us at that moment were outside the legacy of addiction that had controlled so much of our lives. It felt fair that my dad could also know the progress I had known. During the meeting I looked over at my father, though, and noticed that he couldn't stop shaking. He was showing signs of alcohol withdrawals. He had tremors in his hands, and he seemed jumpy and nervous. In the car ride there, I had noticed he looked very ill. He was pale and was thirty pounds lighter. My dad needed to hear so much of what everyone was saying at that meeting, and yet none of it erased the obvious fact that my dad had not chosen to make the beast of addiction powerless or made the choice to end our legacy of addiction. I had done that, and I couldn't do it for him no matter how much I wanted him to know the changes that came after such a success. Life for him on life's terms was still the life of an addict.

The day he left to go back home, we returned to reality. My dad told me that he was so lonely living in the house by himself, and that he didn't have anything to do because he was still not released back to work. He told me that his home was probably going to be foreclosed on, because he didn't have money to pay the mortgage. I asked him to please stay with my fiancé and me for a while. My dad and I had had a great night just before that. Ryan had come over and we had sat on the kitchen counter, keeping my dad company as he cooked us a spaghetti dinner. It was one of the best times that I had had in a very long time. My dad, being the funny guy that he was, had us laughing all night. We didn't want to leave the table, we were laughing so hard that our stomachs hurt. I didn't want him to return to Cottonwood, where none of that was waiting for him. I tried at every step to make my father's life improve. Making his life on my terms didn't work. When I offered to let him stay, he told me that he wanted to get back home, because he was supposed to be starting work again soon. That wasn't true. He wanted to be free to stay addicted.

We compromised by buying him a few toiletries and a couple of cartons of smokes before he left. He asked me for a couple of dollars as well, so that he could buy a few TV dinners to eat once he got back home. I moved into the role of the parent, feeding money to the addict-child. I gave him a hundred dollars because I couldn't bear the thought of him going without. There was a sad mood among us all when my father said goodbye. As I hugged him he squeezed me tighter than he ever had before. It was as if he didn't want the hug to end, so I held on as long as I could. I waved goodbye to him, thinking that might be the last time I ever saw him again. His life could only go on repeating our legacy. He called to say that he had one of the best times in a long time with Ryan and me. I told him once again that I wanted him to stay with me for a while, but I didn't press the issue too much. I told him that I loved him, too, and that I had to let him go, so that I could get to work. I grabbed my cell phone during work the day after that and saw that I had missed four calls from my grandfather in Montana. I instantly knew something was wrong with my dad.

First I tried to call my grandfather, but there was no answer at his house. Before I could call anyone else, I got a call from my mother. She asked me where I was, and I said I was at work. She told me to stay there and that she was on her way, but I wanted to know right then what was going on and argued with her until she would say. My mom hesitantly confessed that my father was dead. I was running through the halls at the bank where I worked after that, and I was crying hysterically, and I remember people stared. I tried to unlock the security door at the back to get to the employee lounge, but I couldn't see through the tears in my eyes. I couldn't stop shaking enough to unlock the door with my keys. A coworker saw me panicking and ran over to let me in. After she let me in, I tried to walk to the lounge, but my legs gave out, and I collapsed to the floor, where I lay and cried and cried. My coworkers knew about the things I faced with my family. Nobody had to ask what happened when they saw me on the floor.

My fiancé arrived soon after. I threw my arms around him and cried even harder. He just held me and let me cry until I could stand on my own. A few minutes later my mother arrived, and we all cried together. I realized that my brother, Ryan, was the only one who hadn't heard. The entire drive to his home, all I could think about was my father. How did he die? I really wanted to know what happened. I dreaded knocking on Ryan's door when we approached it. I hated to tell him that our father had hit the bottom that all of us had hit but decided to let it drop out beneath him and freefall into death. Ryan already knew that with addiction, the choice at the end is always extreme: to recover for good or let the addiction kill you. He saw our tears when he opened the door, and his expression turned to dread. We didn't waste any time telling him what had happened to Dad, and we cried a little more. We all just wanted to know more details, so I called my grandfather to find out how it happened. It wasn't shocking news, but it was painful. My father had shot himself in the head. I wished after hearing that that I could lose myself to the instinct I had to numb myself to everything, but I knew if I did I would end up like my father, and our shared legacy of addiction would be death.

I couldn't believe how overwhelmed I was with grief. It doesn't help to know that an addict is always making choices that may lead to death. I always knew that but still couldn't understand how my father could choose to take his own life. Knowing what can happen to an addict is not the same as understanding why it has to happen, I realized, especially because by then I had been able to change life's terms so that it didn't have to happen to me. I couldn't eat, I couldn't sleep, and I couldn't understand why he killed himself. That dream little girls have about having their father walk them down the aisle had been taken from me just months before I was to be married. This was the time in my life when I really needed a father to share my happiness. I had to have some kind of truth to help sort out my head, so I went to a meeting.

As the meeting started, I didn't say a word about his suicide until it was my turn to speak, but when it was, I broke down and told my story. I was experiencing such stress and such grief that I can't even remember what I said. I was consumed with hopelessness and anger. It had been left up to my brother and me where we wanted to bury my father. After the meeting, I was going to have to sort through the additional emotions of this process. Ryan and I decided that the only thing that felt right was to bury our dad in Montana, alongside my grandmother. She had died by this point, and in Montana my dad could also be buried close to Jason, the brother I never knew. He was the first in our immediate family to die as a result of our family addictions. Attending my father's funeral was the hardest thing that I have ever done. He was the second person to go. Maybe it would have been easier if he had died some other way, a car accident perhaps that wasn't his fault, or from a heart attack. Any ordinary thing would have been better for me than to face the anger I felt at his choice. He took his own life, and we were left to deal with the messy consequences. At the end his own addiction remained the most important thing in his life, and just like always I was a casualty along the way.

This was salt on a fresh wound and almost too much to bear. It felt as if my father had been brutally murdered, except I didn't have anyone to turn my anger toward. He was his own murderer, and his mess spilled over into many lives, from mine to my brother and mother's lives, to the life of my grandfather, and into my world of recovery, into my meetings, into talks with my sponsor, and into the community where I shared my grief.

During this whole time, everyone tiptoed around me. No one knew what to say, so sometimes people didn't say anything at all. My sponsor opened up her home to me in the event I would need her. She helped me do the work I needed to deal with the anger at my dad's addiction, and at addiction as a disease. I had to work through the pain. She helped me learn what my bottom line was with my feelings and helped me to face them and to not run from them. That bottom line was the fact that I never thought that a parent could kill himself. A lot of things in life seemed like an option for even a terrible parent, but not that. My shock to discover that this was not the case was not going to be the thing worth giving up my sobriety for, however. I was determined to not let the tragedy ruin my life. My terms were made to recover. My father's terms for life were made to die.

Addiction is a disease capable of killing anyone. Somewhere in every family legacy, someone has to break the cycle. I am that someone, and so is my mom. Every one of us is that someone when we choose the hope that makes our beast powerless.

PART III.

WATCHING US RECOVER

A Mother-Daughter Guide to Recovery Strategies and Hope

DOES YOUR KID HAVE A DRUG PROBLEM?

CHAPTER 14

AT ONE POINT or another, your kid will be faced with an opportunity to use drugs and will probably be given that opportunity by a friend. At this defining moment, the decision that your child makes is one of the most important, because it may be the choice that changes his or her life forever. Teens often don't see the link between action and consequence, and yet more teens than not repeatedly report that they have experimented with drugs or alcohol. None of us can know who will or will not succumb to addiction, or when. It could be the first time your kid chooses to try drugs that a long-sleeping addiction wakes up and takes hold.

My mom and I woke the beasts of our addictions by abusing alcohol. We did this to numb some sort of pain in life that we didn't want to feel. In this chapter are possible forces, like pain, that may trigger addiction in your child. Of course, no two addictions look identical, but the forces that feed any beast of addiction are similar. You can examine your life for these pressures. After you look for these pressures, the next step that may tell you if your child has a drug problem is looking for physical signs. I have listed the signs my mom could have caught in me if she had known to be looking for these things, or, more important, if she had decided to look for them. Denial will keep any parent from discovering a drug problem that may be right out in the open.

ADDICTIVE FORCES

FAMILY HISTORY: Genetic research shows that 50 percent of the vulnerability to alcoholism is linked to genetics. My mom discovered that my dad's family had an addictive legacy lying one generation back. His parents didn't drink and raised my father using strong morals and standards. She later learned that both of his grandfathers had drinking problems and one of them had owned a bar. Do you know about documented cases of alcoholism in your family lineage? Do you know about addictions that may be one or two generations removed?

FAMILY MODELING: The National Institute on Alcohol Abuse and Alcoholism reports that in addition to the 50 percent of vulnerability to alcohol addiction caused by genetics, 50 percent is triggered by environment. Is your house a culture where heavy drinking is common? Does your child regularly spend time in a culture where heavy drinking is common?

EMOTIONAL ISOLATION: You can't cure a sick brain with a sick brain, my mom says. This basically means that we learn how to cure our hurts by using techniques we have seen. My mom and I both saw sick people around us isolate themselves emotionally to withdraw from feelings that were hard, like pain or shame. We did the same thing before we learned tools to feel these real emotions, because that is what we had been taught. Do you notice that your child is resistant to handling a range of feelings? Are you resistant to a range of feelings?

EXTREME CYCLES: Many addicts have witnessed extreme incidents that end only to see another situation that is equally traumatic. The risk of even one of these incidents would be unlikely in the life of anyone else, much less a string of them. In my family I watched my father marry and divorce several women, be arrested and jailed several times, and attempt several suicides. Do members of your family watch intense things happen multiple times?

PHYSICAL SIGNS OF ADDICTION

When I first started my using, I was smoking pot and drinking. I was always fearful that my mom could tell I was high or drunk. Paranoia may be an easy sign you can spot in your child if something is going on that your child is trying to hide. It is a physical sign of addiction to many types of drugs. For kids who are addicted, it's like their parents can actually read their mind or something, so they will freak themselves out often. They might also freak out if their parents choose to make a straightforward confrontation about their paranoid behavior. When my using began, I started to become very paranoid all the time. The other physical signs I displayed were changes in what I could talk about, objects I began to acquire, smells I created, my ability to keep track of time, and my temper and body.

TALK CHANGES

Talking in a straightforward way will tell you a lot about what is going on with your child, even if you don't ask directly if drug use is going on. I entrenched myself in the world of marijuana smoking and learned from fellow pot smokers the ins and outs of the drug. This meant that I began to know words that I couldn't have otherwise. A few you can listen for are listed here: toke, hay, bud, herb, grass, weed, ganja, cannabis, and Mary Jane. To roll a joint, I had to learn about rolling paper, so I could put the weed in it. If I wanted to cover the smell of my joint, I said I was going to roll a spliff, a half-tobacco, half-weed joint.

I learned a new list of words when I switched my drug to crystal methamphetamine. It was in a class of stimulants that went by a bunch of nicknames on this list: tweak, zip, speed, chalk, Tina, bennies, black beauties, crosses, hearts, L.A. turnaround, truck drivers. If I wanted to do the drug in a smokable form, I had to learn to ask for it by a different nickname, like any of these: ice, crystal, crank, glass, fire, go fast.

All the drugs I did forced me to learn new words, and all drug scenes will teach your teen a vocabulary that you can listen for. My mom may have even succeeded in finding out what I was doing if she had used a keyword from the list below in an unexpected context, because that would have really shocked me. This goes back to the paranoia that will be there in children if they are hiding a problem with drugs. I doubt I could have hidden the terror in my face if I heard my mom say something like, "You know, Lauren, all the robo-tripping that's going on these days is crazy, don't you think?" Here are keywords related to cocaine, heroin, the prescription drug Ritalin, and over-the-counter medicines:

Cocaine goes by coke, C, snow, flake, blow, bump, candy, Charlie, rock, toot, nose candy, he or she, lady flake, liquid lady, nosebleed.

Heroin is sometimes called H, dope, junk, black tar, smack, brown sugar, horse, mud, skag, lady, white girl, goods, Harry.

Ritalin is one drug that represents a new vocabulary that was not really around when I was a drug-addicted teen. It's called vitamin R, R-ball, smart drug, Rits, or West Coast. The newness of this vocabulary is due to the fact that prescriptions are common now for attention deficit/hyperactivity disorder (ADHD) and other behavioral conditions. This happened in Ryan's case. Numerous studies have demonstrated the effectiveness of methylphenidate (or Ritalin) for treatment of ADHD, but it can also be abused as a stimulant. If that's the case, it is easier to listen for the nicknames.

Over-the-counter drugs go by many nicknames because there are so many products that are possible for an addict to get a high from. One craze is for cough syrup. Teens are likely to drink an entire bottle, and NyQuil and Robitussin are brands your child might seek out. Another cold preparation used is Sucrets. It can be crushed and boiled to come up with a powder that contains dextromethorphan, the high that goes by the initials DMX. Code words that apply to this scene are skittling, tussing, skittles, robo-tripping, red devils, velvet, triple C, C-C-C, robotard.

NEW OBJECTS

There are multiple ways that pot can be used, so if you look, you may be able to spot items around your house that you don't recognize. My mom easily found a few of my pipes. Looking around your house will better help you to know if your child is hiding a drug problem. Have you seen anything that looks like the descriptions below?

- BONG: a long cylindrical glass jar where the marijuana smoke is inhaled from the canister.
- PIPE: There are small and big ones; it is basically a tobacco pipe for weed.
- BUBBLER: a type of hand-blown glass pipe that has a pouch for water so that the marijuana smoke filters through the water as it bubbles.
- VAPORIZER: This is a way of smoking weed without any smoke. This machine heats up the marijuana so just the THC is burned off in a vapor and inhaled. This gives out minimal smell and is considered to be better for the lungs.
- EDIBLES: brownies, cookies.
- HOOKAH: Many teens now go to cafés or bars where there are hookahs with flavored, usually fruity tobacco. Teens can buy their

own hookahs and add pot to the flavored tobacco, which covers the scent.

- MEDICINAL: If teens can get their hands on a marijuana prescription, then they can eat marijuana energy bars, pills, and chocolate-infused pot.

Eye drops were constantly with me after I used any of the methods above to do my dope. I had to hide my bloodshot eyes before I came home and had to make eye contact with my mom. I also had pot paraphernalia hidden in my room. This was usually the portable things like rolling papers, lighters, little baggies to bring weed back and forth, my stash of the drug, and pipes. There are pipes available that look like a roll of mints, a makeup brush, a battery, or a cigarette lighter. If you are searching your child's room for paraphernalia, it is wise to keep this in mind and check out anything that does not seem to quite fit with what your child would ordinarily need.

It would have been harder for my mom to look for the evidence of my drug use by the time I was using crystal meth. Amphetamines come in crystals, literally chunks, or a glittery powder that is off-white to yellow in color. You may not be able to spot the chunks or dust. My personal preference was to smoke meth in what is called a glass pipe, but stimulants can also be swallowed in a pill form or snorted in a powder form through the nostrils, where the drug is absorbed into the bloodstream. Needles are also used. If you find a syringe, consider that serious, because it means you may be dealing with an IV drug problem. This will carry serious health risks in addition to the risks of the chemical substance.

DIFFERENT SMELLS

I knew exactly what time my mom got off work, how long it took her to get home, and how long it would take for the garage to air out so that she couldn't smell the weed if I did drugs at home. Right before she would get home is when I would leave the house to go gallivanting around the neighborhood. This aired out my clothes, but just to be sure I would shower myself with perfume or cologne. I also quickly learned to carry gum or mints with me to hide my smell after getting high.

Using stimulant drugs didn't carry as much of a risk that I could be caught by the smell. One thing you may notice is a "fishy" or ammonialike smell if you find the chunks or powder that is used when the drug of choice is crystal meth. If meth is being used in a smokable form, the odor is not distinct enough to notice; you can't place the smell, and it doesn't alarm you.

TIME CHANGES

If I didn't come home after I smoked pot and left my garage to air out, it was because I was going to find my next high. I usually continued my pot smoking down at the park or at a friend's home. This is when I started to miss curfew and skip coming home for dinner. I frequently didn't come home due to the fact that I had gotten too high and was in no condition to come home. Many times I just didn't care, because getting high was way more important than any consequence that I would receive.

When I was smoking crystal meth, I always had time for everything. I would not sleep and would stay up all night in my room while my mom thought that I was fast asleep. There were times that I would stay up anywhere from three to five days at a time. I would continuously clean my room, even down to washing my walls. I would spend hours painting my nails, studying, trying on clothes, grooming myself, and talking on the phone.

DISORDERLY TEMPER

When I would finally come home, my mom usually confronted me with questioning that I knew I just couldn't answer without convicting myself. Her attempts to inquire about any parts of my life made me feel backed into a corner, and I discovered that my best defense was a good offense, by screaming rages and violent outbursts at her. When I felt she was suspicious of my drug using, I became bullying and irritable as a way to intimidate her. She could have looked at the physical toll that was taking on me. The pot smoking made me very tired and worn out, which made me very easy to provoke, and I began to use a lot of profanity to try to get my mom away from me.

My temper totally changed when I started to use crystal meth instead of marijuana. All of a sudden I could carry on hours of conversations with her due to the excessive amount of talking that went with my highs. I realized that she was starting to think that I had really stopped smoking pot because I was so animated, which seemed great. I was no longer avoiding her and would find myself in deep and spiritual conversations about my dreams and life. I was just so energetic that I seemed like a different kid. However, as a user I was driven into a severe depression followed by paranoia and aggression, which is known as "tweaking."

When heavy cocaine users experience paranoia, it almost always disappears once the binge ends. With meth, my severe mood disturbances and bizarre thoughts and behaviors sometimes lasted for days and sometimes for weeks.

BODY SIGNS

I began dropping weight when I started smoking pot because it took up so much of my time. I got extremely hungry only during highs. When my mom was at work, my friends and I would generally be at my house getting high in the garage. Once we were done, we would clean out the refrigerator and go on eating binges. Pot is notorious for causing "the munchies." This cycle of eating may cause the shape of your child's body to fluctuate. You may also notice there is no consistency between the weight of your child and how much food is being consumed at your house. My mom was constantly wondering why one day the refrigerator was completely packed and then the next day it was completely empty.

Using meth was a different story. I dropped an extreme amount of weight in little time due to the fact that I never felt hungry while on meth. I found this to be one of the wonderful side effects of the drug, which just sealed the deal for me that I had found "the perfect drug." My body was in constant motion. When I was coming down off meth I absolutely hated to be in my own skin. I was extremely fatigued and would sleep for endless hours. I was irritable and jittery, and when I would finally wake up after sleeping it off, I would have intense hunger and feel very depressed.

Always look in your child's eyes if you are watching bodily signs.

Dilated eyes are a common side effect of using uppers. When your teen's eyes are dilated, the pupils will appear much larger than usual and may look red or glazed over. Teens who wear sunglasses often, especially at night, may be trying to cover up a problem with uppers.

ADDICTIVE OPTIONS

If you suspect your child is on any kind of drug, first make your expectations for behavior clear. If the problems persist, consult a school guidance counselor or an addiction specialist. If necessary, find a treatment facility that specializes in teen addiction. There are ways to stop this very serious problem in its tracks, but you have to be vigilant. If you have discovered an addiction, you have been vigilant and should feel safer for yourself and your child because recovery is now an option. Next, remain hopeful and take steps as a teammate to your teen. It's essential that a choice to move forward be made. Forcing an addiction to heal is not an option.

ARE YOU ALL READY FOR TREATMENT?

CHAPTER 15

CREATING YOUR TEAM

All I can suggest is that you be open to the possibility of treatment as a family. Lauren believed she could quit on her own. That wasn't a reality. Although many teens believe they can quit on their own, these "self-willed" recoveries usually do not last very long. There are unique problems with teenage and even young adult addicts. First of all, they do not realize the consequences to their health and life that active addiction brings. They feel invulnerable, as if nothing bad will ever happen to them, and they base their decisions on that thinking. So many teens end up losing their life because they don't have the maturity to understand the consequences of feeding their beast of addiction. That is why we need to step in as soon as possible.

I have spoken to parents who are resistant to the idea of treatment because they have already spent so much money on treatment that didn't work for their child. To top that off, many of us have had our money or items stolen by our own teens. Remember, their disease is genetic, and it can skip over your generation and slam into them unexpectedly. This fact may encourage you to see the connection between yourself and your child. Your stories are intertwined. A successful recovery requires the participation of every person in your family who is involved in your story.

The most consistent way addicts have found sobriety is to surround themselves with a group of their sober peers and go to twelve-step meetings on a regular basis. The logical approach for teens to get and stay sober is to be with a group of peers, go to twelve-step meetings, hold each other accountable, and have some fun. It replaces the drug use with a purpose when a group of teens work together on getting and staying sober. A family that mirrors this concept provides a second layer of recovery support. These two layers saved Lauren's life. Recently, she looked at me and said, "Mom, I know for a fact that if it weren't for my recovery, I would either be dead or on the streets today." I also recall a conversation I had with Lauren's former baby sitter several years ago. "You know," she said, "Lauren and I were talking the other day, and she told me that she is so very grateful that you did not give up on her." That gave me all the evidence I need that getting and participating in help for her was the right thing.

What if your child doesn't want help and is unwilling to get into recovery? That is always a possibility. When I walked into my first meeting, I knew that I was exactly where I was supposed to be to get help for myself. Lauren was home playing sick on the couch. There was absolutely nothing I could do to force her to get sober. All I could do was learn how to take care of myself and to accept the help of others who had dealt with the issues I was facing. You will need to be ready to stop enabling your child at this point. By enabling, I mean helping to perpetuate the disease by your actions. The concept of "hitting bottom" means that teens come to realize on their own that their life is not working. I prevented Lauren from realizing this fact by giving her money, rides, and room and board. Of course she didn't want to change while she was receiving this support. After I took the support away, our option for recovery became available when she hit her bottom.

CHOICES FOR EVERYONE

Recovery is a business. You will need to make choices for your family after listening to people that want to sell you their services. The initial person you speak with will most likely be someone who is very good at promoting the services of the program you are researching and at handling your objections. Ask at least the seven questions below to choose a recovery program that all of you can participate in.

1. IS THE PROGRAM SPECIFICALLY DESIGNED FOR ADDICTED ADOLESCENTS?

Most treatment programs are designed for adults. Some programs will include adolescents but usually have only limited activities for the teens. Putting addicted teens into a psychiatric facility is also not a workable solution, as they are grouped with mentally ill teens, which totally distracts from the main issue of addiction.

2. Does the program include treatment for the entire family?

Treatment programs should encourage parents to participate in group meetings, drug education, and counseling. The worst thing for a teen addict in recovery is to have a family that is not recovering. Our home environments will significantly affect the recovery of our kids.

3. How does the program provide aftercare for ongoing recovery?

If our teens have a chance at remaining sober, they must completely change the people they have surrounded themselves with. How are they going to do that if they go away for treatment and return to step right back into their old life? There needs to be a long-term plan that will work.

4. What evidence do you have that your program is successful with young people?

Inquire as to the percentage of teens that complete the program. You can also ask to talk with other parents that have put their teen through the program and perhaps even talk with the teens to ask for their perspective on the experience.

5. DOES THE PROGRAM USE AND PROMOTE TWELVE-STEP RECOVERY?

The twelve steps have been proven to be the most successful way that addicts can maintain long-term recovery. In January 2007, researchers at Stanford University released data that indicated a twelve-step-oriented treatment program that includes attending meetings boosted two-year sobriety rates by 30 percent as compared to cognitive behavioral programs (counseling-based programs).

6. DOES THE PROGRAM UTILIZE MIND- OR MOOD-ALTERING PRESCRIPTION DRUGS?

I caution you to be very careful with this decision. I do not believe it makes sense to treat a drug addict with drugs. It is wise to seek more than one professional opinion regarding your own family choice.

7. WHAT ARE THE PROGRAM RULES AND GUIDELINES?

If the treatment program has rules, they need to be basic and simple. Simple rules make achievements easy to see. The reason that such a program works for teens is because they are able to see hope clearly. Our teens need treatment and recovery from a deadly, complicated disease. In recovery, select something they are attracted to, can get behind quickly, and can become excited about. It is important that the program you select seems attractive to your child.

DO YOU NEED
HELP MANAGING?

CHAPTER 16

HANG IN THERE, PARENTS

I had to think about what I was willing to give up to achieve
recovery for Lauren and myself. When I first began recovery, I can
remember my counselor talking with me about my exhaustion and
what contributed to it. In reviewing my life and schedule, I realized
that I was trying to do it all. I had a demanding full-time job with a
long commute; I did all of the cooking, cleaning, laundry, and shopping for our family; I was involved in church activities and ran the
children to school functions, gymnastics, and karate. My life was
so incredibly unmanageable; it was a true juggling act just trying to

keep all of the balls in the air. I prioritized by price-tagging my time, working clutter control, and speaking up.

PRICE-TAGGING YOUR TIME: Write down all the weekly activities in your life and rate them by importance. Then, consider alternatives to some of the activities that consume the most time. For me these were basic tasks, like the six hours per week I spent cleaning the house. I realized that I made a good income and could certainly afford to have someone help me with the heavy cleaning. I also made a decision to move closer to work, which cut down my commute time, when I recognized that my commute was consuming a good deal of hours every week.

The most important activities in your recovery will require the most time and money. To save both, I had to make changes. Paying for recovery for us was a central issue. I chose to put a second mortgage on my house to pay for treatment. One month later, I got a big raise, and I saved that money to cover the costs we had that related to recovery. In less than a year I was able to pay for the treatment that helped save my teen's life.

Are any of the suggestions on the list below an idea that your family can use to save time or money?

• Hire help for household cleaning
• Give up activities not vital to recovery
• Cut down on work or overtime
• Reduce television watching
• Delegate chores within the family
• Consider carpooling options

- Shop online for grocery delivery
- Solicit baby-sitting from family/friends
- Limit the length of phone calls
- Relocate
- Stop worrying and procrastinating
- Start taking action

WORKING CLUTTER CONTROL: My physical space and my emotional space both required organizing. I was always spending time looking for things that I had misplaced. This enhanced my feelings that my life was out of control.

To calm my physical space, I began a routine of planning for the next action. This included my home and office. I started putting my dirty clothes in the hamper instead of on the bed or floor, for example, and I put the dishes in the dishwasher instead of leaving them in the sink. I even started making to-do lists as a memory technique. I didn't have to constantly try to remember what the next action in a given time was.

To calm my emotional space, I began a system of boundaries against "high drama" connections. This included thoughts and people that caused me to wallow in negative feelings. I started letting go of any thought about being disorganized, being indecisive, worrying, and not knowing my priorities if the thought did not connect to an action I could take to change my circumstance. If I could not take an action to help a friend change a circumstance, I also started letting go. I realized I had been spending hours on phone calls about unchanging soap operas.

SPEAKING UP: Acknowledge the fact that your child has a serious disease and has spun out of control because of it. This will be a major challenge due to embarrassment or a different emotion that you may associate with addiction having taken over your family. Please consider the fact that we did not cause that and we cannot let any shame we may feel cause us to try to hide the truth from those who are close to us.

I have found that the direct approach works best with relatives and friends. Before I chose to speak up, I was using time and energy to hide my situation. After, I found that people close to me had already sensed there was something going wrong. Many times they were able to be supportive and understanding given the chance to understand. I have provided a sample conversation here that you can use to approach relatives and friends. Keep it simple. It is not necessary to go into an extensive dialogue about the details of everything that led up to the addiction.

YOU: "This is a bit difficult for me, but I need to talk with you about Lauren. We recently discovered that she has a major problem with drug addiction. We are doing everything we can to try to help her, and she entered a treatment facility this week. We could use your support and your prayers for our family right now."

To avoid feeling pressured to give a reply, offer this basic response if you are met with further questions you do not feel comfortable answering at that time.

YOU: "I am having a rough time right now and would prefer to not get into the details."

To approach an employer, coworker, teacher, counselor, or other professional involved in your family life, modify the sample conversation above using the following considerations:

- In dealing with bosses or coworkers, it is best to try to keep your personal life out of the work situation if you can.
- Some people feed off drama and gossip.
- It may become necessary to share your plan for recovery with a boss or coworkers if it will affect your work schedule.
- If you remain open to hearing a person out, this will allow you to gather information and facts.
- Experts can only help up to the level of what they know and how they have been trained to handle issues. It is important for you to educate yourself independently.
- Confrontation was not as bad as I thought it would be. I was a stronger person than I thought I was.

HANG IN THERE, TEENS

Social pressure for teens is intense. Teens have to wear the right clothes, own the coolest gadgets, have a cell phone, Twitter, and blog and be on Facebook or MySpace. When terrible situations arise and peer pressure kicks in so badly that you want to return to your addiction, that moment can make you forget you will have to live with the choice that you make in that second for the rest of your life.

I found many situations on my journey to recovery during which I made poor decisions that were contrary to my character and beliefs. I found that I was setting myself up for failure because I was choosing the wrong kind of support system. Sometimes I even chose the right support system but the wrong people to rely on in that system. I was clueless of where and whom to turn to, or how to match the two things up. Turn to one of the places I talk about here if you are also feeling pressure. You can learn from the mistakes I made and select supportive people at supportive places you can go to during your recovery that will help you hang in there during intense times.

CHURCH: I thought that when I went to church I would find support with my peers, but instead I found that many of them were living the same type of lifestyle that I was. I repeated my habit of finding the people that used. This led to the need for me to lie at church, and the lies just grew and grew. I would tell my church counselors that I was finally free of drugs and alcohol, which led them to ask me to speak about my addiction during a service in front of the whole congregation. I spoke for ten minutes one time about how my religion saved me from my beast. All the while the party friends I had were laughing hysterically in the crowd because they knew I was lying about my sobriety. The attention didn't support my recovery because it was supporting my addiction to feeling accepted and important instead.

RELATIONSHIPS: When I began my romantic relationship with John, I had an inescapable desire to present myself to him in the most positive light. Doing this halted my own personal honesty in my recovery process because all my focus turned to the infatu-ation of this new relationship between us. This distraction while in drug treatment had negative effects on my recovery process. Even though this distraction felt compelling and right, it ultimately was toxic to my recovery. In the end the relationship was just two people going back and forth, enabling each other to stay unhealthy, and ultimately putting their sobriety at risk.

MEETINGS/GROUP/RECOVERY: Before I began going to recovery, I was so embedded with the message that there was no hope that I constantly played up the victim role. In recovery I began to try out new behaviors, like honesty and letting people in. I was given the tools to start taking positive risks, and I found that I had started receiving more self-knowledge and that I had more to offer to others than I had ever believed was possible. Once I decided to give the sober thing a try and got a few months of sobriety under my belt, I found myself in an enormous emotional transition. The support I had found at recovery gave me the assistance and encour-agement that I needed during this stage when I began to salvage my life. I was able to enjoy the companionship and support of people that understood and empathized with me at each new step.

ARE YOU DOING WHAT WORKS?

CHAPTER 17

NAVIGATING LIFE WITH an addicted child in the family creates havoc in the house because there are a number of parenting strategies that just plain do not work. This chapter lists those broken strategies so that you can reflect on your own life and determine if you are doing what works or what does not. More-effective parenting options are the ultimate goal; however, the strategies that work cannot begin to take effect until you identify the broken dynamics presently at work in your home, your child, yourself, or a combination of these three.

DENIAL THAT YOUR CHILD IS USING

A parent is unfortunately often the last to know, or the last to acknowledge, the fact that a child has become an addict. Our tendency is to explain away odd behavior that should set off red flags. Some explanations we may offer on our child's behalf are "They're just doing a little partying" or "I did it when I was a kid, and I turned out okay." These are safe-mode thoughts that keep us protected from the truth and from facts that we are not ready to deal with yet. Denial is a stall tactic, plain and simple. Eventually addiction will be necessary to face, admit, and deal with.

When I first heard how serious Lauren's drug problem was, I thought my friend Shirley was just making the problem up to make her own daughter, Lindsey, look good. My brain cycled back to this blame on Shirley. I wanted to find any way possible to justify the idea that things for Lauren were not really as bad as what I had heard from my friend. The interesting thing is that my behavior toward Shirley was quite similar to the denial of an addict who refuses to admit that a substance abuse problem exists. This does not help your child, to discount the reality that an addiction has taken hold. Addiction is a serious illness, and your child is at risk. We can't decrease this risk by blaming someone else or creating a plausible excuse for a problem that is way bigger than us that we can't control, change, or stop without help.

The best thing we can do is come out of denial to seek the help we need. Things will not work themselves out. The hope is that the sooner we come to this realization and start to seek this help, the sooner we can begin finding solutions that work.

PERSONAL GUILT

One struggle we share as parents is personal blame over the choices our kids have made. Sure, we could have been more available or nurturing or less critical. Perhaps we should have been more of a parent to our children and less of a friend or vice versa. Single parents are especially hard on themselves for not being more present or not providing constant supervision. Married parents often blame the problems of the marital relationship for affecting an addicted kid, or even worse, spouses end up blaming one another for what has happened with their child. Addiction is at the core of any of these types of blame and causes one of two effects that are both counterproductive to parenting strategies that work.

First, the "blame game" begins when we accept responsibility for our child's addiction, because this may increase our denial of the problem, as we find it difficult to face an addiction we feel we may have caused. Our kids will fan this feeling along if we let them. Teen drug abusers frequently blame a parent as one main reason the addiction began in the first place. It just gives our teens justification to continue their behavior if we play the "blame game" and makes it very difficult for them to find recovery.

Second, the blame game keeps us paralyzed with feelings of unrealistic guilt. It's extremely damaging to our entire families to remain stalled in tremendous levels of guilt, and it fuels teenage addicts by coddling them. It doesn't change or help the situation, which is the ultimate goal, to replace self-blame and guilt with a parenting strategy that works.

ALLOWING THE SITUATION TO GET OUT OF HAND

Taking control of the situation with your addicted child as soon as possible is essential. Denial and the blame game must be defeated to stop situations from escalating.

By not dealing with things early on, we will discover that the small problems escalate to larger ones. The teen may end up suspended from school, as I experienced with Lauren and Ryan, which can lead to increasingly complicated situations like police involvement, arrest, dealing drugs, running away, attempting suicide, or all of these things. Out of denial or guilt we may tolerate bad behavior at any of the early stages in this sequence. This is unacceptable if we expect the situations to end, because emotional ties to our children are manipulating us into tolerance for addiction rather than delivering us toward a solution to addiction that will take control of the situation at hand.

An addicted child is at risk for insanity, death, or suicide. It is important to be clear that any of these ends are the realistic situation that awaits you and your child if the disease of addiction is left untreated. Most parents do not want to place their child into treatment and may end up doing so out of sheer desperation, but contrast this against the realities that await an addict after situations are allowed to escalate. Placement into treatment is a better option because it can save the life of your kid. Continued addiction, parental guilt, the blame game, or paralysis due to personal grief only allows the disease to continue in your child and to escalate, always leading to extremely negative ends.

ENABLING

Enabling parents are those that prioritize the comfort of their child over the addiction that has taken hold of the child's life. Many times we are enabling parents without even knowing it. I provided a home of course for my family, but I was also continuing to allow Lauren and Ryan to use the TV, cell phones, and computers, and I was offering them an allowance. Tough Love techniques taught me to consistently cut these enabling behaviors off because the fact was that I had actually been achieving the opposite result of what I wanted. I wanted good things for Lauren and Ryan, and I strove to love, protect, and provide for them, but before I stopped enabling I was definitely hurting them by allowing the addictions to continue.

To draw the line against enabling, it is necessary to recognize where enabling begins. As parents, our children depend on us for food, shelter, health, and emotional support. Beyond those things it is possible to begin enabling, by which I mean helping to perpetuate the disease of addiction through our actions. Lauren, for example, was going over to another area of town to visit her drug dealer boyfriend and other drug-using friends every day, including weekends. Oftentimes I would give her a ride to this area of town because that was where she went to school, but then I found myself willing to give her a ride there on the weekends as well. Now, why would I give her a ride somewhere if I knew she was in that part of town killing herself with drugs? There is no logical answer. That is an example of enabling, then, because my need to be "nice" to my daughter took priority over the dangerous reality of the situation at hand.

By ending your enabling patterns, you help your child hit bottom and also help yourself. Refusing to enable addiction announces the fact that in our homes we do not accept unacceptable behavior. Illegal drug and alcohol use is unacceptable. The message that we want to give our children consistently is that we love them, we want the best for them, and we are on their side, but we will not contribute favors that make addiction a possible lifestyle choice.

NOT SETTING LIMITS

It is important that we have rules and boundaries in our home, and it is especially key that we communicate these rules to our children. In addition, rules require a support system outside the home that will reinforce consequences for our kids and provide us with strength to maintain the limits we set down. Setting limits alone, with no support system and no professional help, is dangerous and does not work. The dangers involve an enormous loss of personal energy and conflict with our teens that escalate into anger, turmoil, arguments, tears, and reoccurring feelings of guilt, denial, self-blame, grief, or all of these.

Eventually I came to realize I had not set limits, nor set them clearly, for Lauren and Ryan. What I had done was discuss limits. This is different from setting limits clearly. I took offense when my sponsor pointed out that I had played a part in allowing many situations to escalate. I was the parent, I was informed, and if my daughter was yelling at me, I should not allow myself to be upstaged by somebody in a training bra and braces. With this insight, I felt I had nothing to lose if I began to set limits differently. It didn't take long before things started to change once I was willing to set a limit and walk away without negotiating with my children or choosing to listen to hysteria, whining, or tantrums.

To follow through with the boundaries I set for Lauren and Ryan, I needed the strong support of my recovery group, my sponsor, and my significant other. My boyfriend, Bob, was a key supporter of mine. He attended meetings with me, and we stood strong together when we went through the tough times, which presented a united front against Lauren and Ryan. I did not stand against my children alone when setting limits. This was essential because a child will attempt to divide and conquer two adults that set limits.

Bob and I also learned that "no" is a complete sentence. Negotiating a limit with your teen does not work. Talking leads to discussion, which can quickly be flipped by your child into an interrogation about your parenting methods, when the real discussion is about the unacceptable behavior of your child. You do not have to be interrogated or go into volumes of explanations about limits. They are reasonable and necessary. End the discussion, and walk away if you haveto, to preserve the limits you set.

NOT TALKING TO OUR KIDS
ABOUT SUBSTANCE ABUSE

In 2005, the Office of National Drug Control Policy stated, "Significant parental involvement" is the most important factor in deterring young people from using drugs. Little changes each time a similar survey of teens is conducted about the role a parent plays in shaping the choice that a child makes regarding substance abuse. Adolescents whose parents talk to them on a regular basis about substance abuse and genetic predispositions are 42 percent less likely to use drugs; however, the Partnership For A Drug-Free America finds that only one in four teens reported having these conversations. Can you imagine how much drug usage statistics could drop if 100 percent of parents talked to their children? Maybe you are one of those parents whose children have not yet experimented with drugs. If so, it does not work to remain silent. You have an unbelievable opportunity.

There are a number of reasons that parents don't talk to teens about substance abuse, but it is important that we get beyond any justification for remaining silent. What works is just talking about it anyway. It will be uncomfortable, and it may be realistic to believe we are jeopardizing the relationship with our child, yet as parents we are ultimately responsible for the welfare and safety of our teens. It is crucial that we do whatever they need to become educated. Sometimes this will feel as if your teen is not listening to you; however, it is indicated in survey after survey that this fact is wrong. Your child really does take things that you say seriously and to heart when you talk to him or her.

WHAT IS STILL GOING ON?

CHAPTER 18

PARENTS ARE STILL a teen's greatest influence. It is an overwhelming blow to this fact if you realize that your teen may be dabbling in drugs and alcohol or has a full-blown addiction. Trust me, though, a parent is so influential. My mom let my behaviors slide and was denying obvious indications of drug use in our house. The message I received from her choices was that I could still get away with a lot because she couldn't catch me. The longer you deny, the longer you wait, the more your teen, you, and your family will suffer. Parents need to know that all users—yes, even your child—will be working overtime to cover their behavior. Lying is a big part of the disease.

To find out what is still going on, consider each of the scenarios in this chapter against the daily lifestyle at your house.

THE SCENE: *New, older friends keep showing up.*
WHAT'S STILL GOING ON: *Contact with drug buddies.*

When children become involved in using and selling drugs, their circle of friends will change drastically. The crowd that you once knew and trusted will be nowhere to be found. When Ryan and I met an older man in our neighborhood in Colorado who dealt weed, we knew we had hit the jackpot. He was married, yet had a thing for younger girls. I had him eating out of the palm of my hand. For months before I moved back to Arizona, I would spend countless hours at his home getting high for free.

Meeting the friends your child keeps is essential. Also, meeting the parents can tell you a lot about any teen and help you keep close tabs on yours. You might even consider calling or getting together regularly to share information with other parents about how your children behave, what they like to do, and any changes you've noticed lately.

THE SCENE: *Money doesn't seem to be a problem.*
WHAT'S STILL GOING ON: *Theft, bartering.*

I found out early on in my using that some drugs are even cheaper and easier to obtain than alcohol. The dealer pushes the drugs for cheap, and once the teen is hooked, the dealer then raises the price or sometimes asks for a sexual favor in return for the next high. Drugs are an expensive habit otherwise, which means that an addicted teen must begin to steal or otherwise barter anything to get money or access to substances.

Once my mom realized that Ryan and I were indeed smoking pot and drinking alcohol, and that none of our chores were being done, she decided that she would no longer give us money. This was the correct choice. She was not going to be an active participant in our drug purchases anymore. The consequence of that choice was that Ryan and I then had to figure out ways that we could still get money to support our pot smoking addiction because neither one of us had hit our bottom and was ready to quit using.

We decided that we would sneak out at night to break into neighborhood cars. Theft is what we turned to when we were desperate. We would dress in all black and wait for our parents to go to sleep, and then meet to scrounge up whatever valuables we could find in the vehicles we hit. People didn't lock their car doors as often as they do now, so it was easy to find many cars to steal from. We found wallets with money, but even just an ashtray full of change was worth robbing the car for. We took purses, clothing, and guns and sold what we could for drug money.

There were also times when I dealt drugs to make money. I brought LSD into a rehab center with me to sell to other patients for more than the price I was able to buy it for. I used the benefit I had as an outpatient to score drugs when I was not at the program. In my own neighborhood I sold to younger kids because I knew they would never notice I was tricking them. I made bags of my mom's spices that looked like bags of weed, and when the younger kids would call and ask to get drugs, I took their money and went to purchase my own real stash.

THE SCENE: *The house is empty during part of the day.*
WHAT'S STILL GOING ON:
Partying, drug sales/exchanges, planning.

Keeping your home open and available to your teen and your teen's friends will certainly give you a window to notice any new behaviors that may arise. We had kids living in the rafters of our garage. These were friends that had been kicked out of their homes or just simply run away. Ryan and I used this as a means of extorting them for their drugs, or we made them go steal alcohol for us in return for a warm place to sleep. Our mom had set up a couch in our garage, which just ended up giving us a warm place to get high when she was away from the house, instead of freezing our butts off outside to hide from her in the cold and snowy winter months in Colorado.

Neighborhood friends began to use our house as a base. If they wanted to get high, they knew they could just come to our garage, hang out, and use. It was easy for friends to come and go through the garage into the house. If your child is using or has friends that use, take all your valuables out of the home, or they will probably be stolen if you are not home for several hours a day. Don't leave your wallet or purse lying around, especially your bank checks.

THE SCENE: *Online shopping.*
WHAT'S STILL GOING ON: *Drug research.*

Teens can now use the Internet to buy prescription drugs. This has made the drug menu bigger, because hundreds of online pharmacies sell medications with no questions asked and no prescription necessary. Painkillers, depressants, antianxiety meds, and stimulants are easy to order and learn more about online. One big problem with prescription drug use is that a teen may not realize that there is very little difference between the amount of medication that can produce a high and the amount that can cause an overdose. Prescription drugs are just as dangerous as illicit drugs.

You can monitor Internet use of your credit and debit cards and investigate packages addressed to your child that arrive in the mail. You can also monitor the types of websites that your child visits by using the history function of your web browser or a program that will do this for you invisibly. Thanks to the Internet, teens can exchange drug information with anyone around the world, so the drug scene today is constantly changing. Parents need to be constantly updating their knowledge of teen drug abuse and the new "now" drugs. Don't feel uneasy with these tactics. Your child will be using a cell phone and the Internet to constantly learn better ways to deceive you.

THE SCENE: *Constant coming and going, isolation at home.*
WHAT'S STILL GOING ON: *Home use.*

When I was using, I didn't even want to come home for dinner, and when I was home I was sure to stay as far away from my mom as possible to avoid having to answer uncomfortable questions. Your teen will stay away from your house as much as possible while using because it is not connected to the party scene, dealers, or using friends. Eventually your child will come for something. When your child does come home, what has been going on will be obvious. If your kid comes in with friends and they are particularly ravenous or giggly, you should suspect that they have been smoking pot.

Teens who are involved with drugs will probably be spending the majority of their time away from family and refuse to participate in family activities, so be aware when a desire for privacy develops into isolation. When I was grounded or stuck in the house, I found ways to get high while in the home. Many times I would say I was taking a shower, and I would take my pot into the bathroom. I would stuff a towel under the door and stand on the toilet to blow the smoke into the bathroom fan up in the ceiling. Then I would take my shower as normal, which would cover up the smell of the pot smoke. When I would get high in my room, I would also use empty toilet paper rolls and stuff them with dryer sheets and blow my pot smoke through the roll so that it came out covering up the smell. Another trick is the use of incense.

ARE YOU AWARE OF THESE RESOURCES?

CHAPTER 19

THE TWELVE-STEP PROGRAM

The history of the twelve steps is a fascinating story. Two desperate drunks who met in Akron, Ohio, founded Alcoholics Anonymous (AA), the first twelve-step program, back in 1935. One had been a Wall Street big shot and the other a surgeon. At the time there had been no known cure for their addiction, and most alcoholics ended up in jails, institutions, or morgues.

Both men had tried many ways to stop drinking and had been hospitalized numerous times. They were both at a place where they felt they were beyond help. Then a miracle happened. In getting to know each other, they began to realize that by helping each other, they were both able to stay sober. The twelve steps were adopted, and within a few short years, there was a documented success rate of over 75 percent for the pioneer groups that sprang up around the country.

The twelve steps were written from experience and not as a theory. A tradition was born within the "anonymous" twelve-step programs of using only first names. Bill W., one of the founders, said many times that nobody invented AA. Bill often revealed that everything in the program was borrowed from medicine, religion, and experience. The main thing about it was that it worked.

THE TWELVE STEPS

1. We admitted we were powerless over alcohol—that our lives had become unmanageable.
2. Came to believe that a Power greater than ourselves could restore us to sanity.
3. Made a decision to turn our wills and our lives over to the care of God as we understood Him.
4. Made a searching and fearless moral inventory of ourselves.
5. Admitted to God, to ourselves, and to another human being the exact nature of our wrongs.
6. Were entirely ready to have God remove all these defects of character.
7. Humbly asked Him to remove our shortcomings.
8. Made a list of all persons we had harmed, and became willing to make amends to them all.

9. Made direct amends to such people wherever possible, except when to do so would injure them or others.

10. Continued to take personal inventory and when we were wrong promptly admitted it.

11. Sought through prayer and meditation to improve our conscious contact with God as we understood Him, praying only for knowledge of His will for us and the power to carry that out.

12. Having had a spiritual awakening as the result of these steps, we tried to carry this message to alcoholics, and to practice these principles in all of our affairs.

A SAMPLE RECOVERY MAP: LAUREN

Bottoming out is crucial for addicts, because if they can function as normal people for years, addicts will see no reason to quit using the drugs or alcohol. I wasn't ready to get sober until I found that my life had gotten bad enough to make the change. I entered the residential house at the twelve-step center due to the fact that my meth dealer went to prison and my mom would not allow me to stay in her home if I continued to use.

There is no way to force a teenager into addiction treatment. Some parents actually hire third-party professionals called interventionists to come to their home and lead their family through the process. Sometimes the family doctor can help with a referral. Some families unite with their teens' friends to intervene as a group. This was the case with me. Lindsey confronted her mom about my problem, which led to my mother confronting me. A group of people were worried I was going to die at the point when I hit my bottom.

Once I finally entered the residential house, I was able to get away from all the people in my life that enabled my addictions. I was embarrassed at the fact that I was, once again, in another rehab; however, the residential house focused on teen drug abuse and knew how to give me, as a teen, the right tools to fight my kind of addiction. I abused multiple substances, while adults may be more singular in their focus. I didn't discriminate against any drug. If I never used it, it was simply due to the fact that it never crossed my path.

About ten days into my residential treatment, I made a decision to leave and experienced a relapse. This ended up being my moment of clarity, as I realized that I was standing directly at a fork in the road. I was finally involved with a treatment program that focused on teenage addiction, and I knew the program was giving me tools to start a new life. I was in intense group therapy six hours a day prior to my relapse. My knowledge of my using and myself had already begun to change by the time I ran away from the residential house. My head was filled with so much positive healing at that time, but it was in transition against my disease, which was grasping at anything it could to feed itself and stay alive.

There is a saying, "A head full of program and a belly full of booze do not mix." This is what happened to me during my relapse. It resulted in a bad high for me, and I ultimately made the decision at Steve's house to leave and see the recovery process through because counselors were successfully rewiring my thinking. They had not only addressed my substance abuse but also helped me to navigate finding my own identity that I was neglecting while addicted to the drugs and alcohol. I began to find alternative methods of dealing with my negative thinking, my depression, and my mood swings.

I had no effective problem-solving and social skills and needed to be taught to build my self-esteem when I began recovery at the twelve-step center. I didn't trust anyone, and I had to start learning how to put trust in others once again. I was shown the tools and given the verbal skills of how to ask for help if I needed it, yet it was up to me to practice these tools regularly and consistently. I was never willing to do that before. I had to start to learn how to accept life on life's terms and decide for myself where and when to apply the correct tools. Of course, once I graduated from the program, I was frightened. I had to find a new group of peers and a support system for myself. I knew that I could not give in to the misconception that I was now healed, because in recovery we believe that we are never fully recovered but are simply recovering.

Graduating from the program, I chose to follow up with twelve-step meetings that I continue with today. I have also continued with the sponsor I met in recovery. This support was essential to face a major trauma I had as a sober adult. I hit an all-time low in my life after my father shot and killed himself due to his own addictive relapse. This happened when I had five years sober, and I felt the anxious beast in me waiting to use that event as an opportunity to draw me into the family legacy I had chosen to break.

It was the most horrendous situation that had ever happened in my life. I could have easily played up the victim role; however, I had been diligent at setting myself up with a tremendous support system through my sponsor, my meetings, and my peers. I threw myself into as many meetings as possible. For a good month, I constantly surrounded myself with loved ones and support from friends. I allowed myself to experience all the stages of grieving for my dad and allowed my emotions to be released through talking and writing about his suicide so that I did not repress my feelings.

I guess I never thought my father would kill himself. A lot of things in life seem like an option, but that never seemed possible. I never thought I would have to deal with suicide ever in my lifetime, and yet after I had to deal with it, the tragedy did not become the thing worth giving up my sobriety for. I was determined not to let the impossible choice of my father ruin my life, and instead I kept it with me as a reminder that the disease of addiction is capable of killing loved ones.

Since the tragedy of my father's death, I have married the man of my dreams, and together we have two children. At times, I get to see glimpses of their grandfather in each of them. I credit a strength and a higher power I found through twelve-step for the ability to move through my pain when it rises and, instead of breaking, to continue on with my life. My father was not there that day to walk me down the aisle, but I know the spirit of my dad was with me and continues to be with me at all the great moments I will experience.

My family has been ravaged by the disease of addiction, and I am unwilling to be a victim of it anymore. Most of my healing came to me through working the steps, which encouraged me to share my story, and in turn I got to help others that share the same history I have. From this I have been given more power to walk strong in my own life, to fight my own battles, because somewhere in every legacy of addiction, someone has to break the cycle. Why not me, and why not now?

ONLINE EDUCATION

DO IT NOW FOUNDATION, drug fast fact cards: www.doitnow.org/pages/fastfacts.html

NATIONAL INSTITUTE ON DRUG ABUSE: www.nida.nih.gov

PARENTS. THE ANTI-DRUG: www.theantidrug.com

TWELVE STEP, ALCOHOLICS ANONYMOUS: www.aa.org

THE NATIONAL CENTER ON ADDICTION AND SUBSTANCE ABUSE AT COLUMBIA UNIVERSITY: www.casacolumbia.org

THE PARTNERSHIP FOR A DRUG-FREE AMERICA: www.drugfree.org

TEEN DRUG ABUSE: www.teen-drug-abuse.org

A current list of resources can be found on our website at www.addictedlikeme.com

ACKNOWLEDGMENTS

WE WANT TO THANK our agent, Barbara Poelle, who enthusiastically believed in our work and never gave up when the going got tough. Also, thank you to our editor Katie Meier, who has helped us take our book from good to great.

Much gratitude to Nancy Diluca, Sheri Greenawalt, and Tiffanie Burrey for their constant encouragement and to Susan Cox and Sue Swannack for their generous time and service.

Thank you to Ryan, who graciously allowed his story to be a part of this book. Without you, this book wouldn't be all that it is meant to be. Deepest gratitude to Papa, who has continuously been the rock of our family.

We are sincerely grateful to our husbands, Bob Franklin and Mike King, for supporting us. We love you both.

To Bob M. (you know who you are), who was key to our sobriety: Never forget all of the good that you have done. We also wish to thank all of the people in recovery that we have met along the way that have enriched our lives by unselfishly sharing their experience, strength, and hope.

Finally, a word of deep love and appreciation to Rose Osburne, who told us years ago that this book was meant to be written and shared with others so that our message of hope could be heard.

ABOUT THE AUTHORS

© TIFFANIE BURREY

KAREN FRANKLIN has spent the past twenty-one years recovering from the legacy of her family addiction. She has committed her life to helping others in their personal recovery process. Karen resides in Phoenix, Arizona, with her husband and two dachshunds. She is an avid reader, hiker, scuba diver, and nature lover. Karen has spent twenty-five years in the information technology field and has volunteered since 1989 in facilitating weekend recovery workshops for adults and teens dealing with grief. This is her first book, and Karen plans to continue writing to produce more nonfiction books on recovery issues.

LAUREN KING has spent the past eleven years living a sober life. She has a wealth of experience to share that can help parents of teen addicts to understand adolescent addiction. Lauren is happily married, living in Surprise, Arizona, and is the mother of two beautiful girls. She is currently pursuing a degree in chemical dependency. Lauren has spent her sober years working tirelessly to help others break from addictive family legacies by passing on the gift of sobriety that she has earned. This is her first book. Lauren plans to continue writing on recovery from addiction.

PLEASE VISIT WWW.ADDICTEDLIKEME.COM FOR MORE INFORMATION AND UPDATES.

DISCUSSION QUESTIONS

1. Describe how history repeats itself with Karen and Lauren's individual stories of addiction? What are some of the most striking parallels?

2. Do you think it is possible that alcohol and drug use could have been prevented if Karen or Lauren had been informed and educated about the "family secrets" regarding the genetic history of substance abuse in their family?

3. What were some of the warning signs that Lauren and Ryan were using? Would it have made a difference if Karen had intervened at an earlier time?

4. Lauren's drug use started innocently with curiosity and wanting to fit in. How do you think it happened that this young girl, who was so against drug and alcohol use, could have been so easily overtaken by addiction?

5. Did the peer pressure or the move to Colorado play a part in Lauren's decision to use drugs? Could she have avoided getting into drugs if she had gotten involved in other activities? What could Lauren have done differently to make friends? How do you deal with difficult feelings or situations?

6. What methods did Lauren use to hide her addiction from her mother? How do you feel that Lauren's addiction alienated her from her mom?

7. Discuss Lauren's progression of doing more harmful drugs as her disease of addiction escalated. What was the attraction of crystal meth for Lauren? How did it hurt her? Do you think her progression is typical of most people who start abusing drugs and alcohol?

8. Denial is a common theme for family members of addicts. How important was it that Karen came out of denial about the addiction in her children?

9. Karen's friend Shirley and Lauren's teen friends Lindsey and Paige played a major role in Lauren's coming to the end of her crystal meth usage. Do you think they contributed to saving Lauren's life? What would you say or do if you had a friend in the same situation?

10. What might the result have been if Lauren had not been willing to take an honest look at her life and realize she

needed to get sober? What do you think were the biggest factors that led to her decision?

11. What were some of the things that were different about the twelve-step program that Lauren attended as opposed to some of the other programs she had been exposed to? What do you think made the biggest difference in Lauren's success in the program?

12. Why do you think Lauren had to change so many things in her life when she entered recovery? Did it work and was it worthwhile? How do you think things would have played out differently had Lauren gone back to her old friends when she completed her inpatient recovery?

13. The fact that Lauren did not relapse during the breakup with her boyfriend and her miscarriage is significant. What do you think contributed to her strength during that difficult time?

14. One of the points stressed in the book is that parents need to educate themselves and take action. What was the impact on Karen's family as she worked to gain knowledge, seek help, and take action around her children's addiction?

15. How will teens who read Lauren's story be impacted? Do you feel her story could act as a deterrent for kids considering alcohol or drug usage?